*I dedicate this book to my sons Bryn and Louie,
my nephew Luca, my granddaughters Willow and Violet,
and to all those made homeless due to
the bushfires of 2019-2020.*

'This book is a work of art, in so many ways and on so many levels. Milena Cifali bravely traces the losses of the summer of 2020 in a deeply personal account that resonates across time and space. Geographically located in a world that has changed forever, this book is a timely reminder that the work of mourning is also the work of restoration, and there is much work ahead of us. Her courage and resilience pave the way.'

Carolyn Minchin, Master of Social Work

'Amidst the background of the recent fires that devastated Australia's east coast, and then the social dislocation of the Coronavirus, Milena Cifali, having lost her home to the fire in Mallacoota has created a meditation on life, loss, and renewal. This is a poignant account of the thoughts and emotions that flare up and affect the soul when one's home has been taken away. All through this moving account is a yearning for 'home' and a search for connection, and always the restorative power of music and story telling.'

Jim Sakkas, prize winning author and Mallacoota resident

'Milena Cifali documents a bleak, bewildering time in Australian history. *Mallacoota Time* shows that it is possible to find great light after an upheaval, even a toppling into the void. Milena reminds us—right when we need to hear it—that people are fundamentally empathetic and generous. A moving, raw and deeply honest work.'

Lorne Johnson, teacher and poet, June, 2020

'Remembering Mallacoota, Milena Cifali not only processes her own grief at the loss of her home but articulates the emotions of many who were scarred by Australia's vicious bushfires. In poetic language, she evokes a lost world of beloved wildlife and creativity on her verandah.

'In an age when we are all so busy and self-obsessed, this is an eye-opening, heart-wrenching read for anyone who can make room for empathy. Milena shows that painful as it is, you have to lose absolutely everything in order to start a new life.'

Helen Womack, international journalist, Budapest

'There is a light in every dark cavern if we have eyes to see it. Milena's light is in her action—she has turned adversity into art. She has turned destruction into creation. That which fuelled the pyre of her comfort has launched her into a new life.'

Graeme Morris, music teacher, guitarist, lover of life

'The tragic fires of the Summer of 2020, back-to-back with the world-wide threat of the Coronavirus pandemic, is the subject of *Mallacoota Time*. Milena takes the reader on a personal journey that explores the concepts of change, loss and a sense of belonging. In the final analysis, it confirms the healing and uplifting nature of music, art and the importance of human empathy in finding the courage to face adversity.

'Milena's narration is raw, emotive and immediate and we are swept along with her, immersed in her quest to come to terms with sudden, shattering developments. The reading of this book may well help us to mould our own understanding of our sense of home and belonging.'

Eleni Roumeliotis, English Teacher.

First Published in 2020 by Echo Books

Echo Books is an imprint of Jenkins Family Nominees Pty Ltd, ABN 14 640 032 604

Registered Office: 5/5 Markeri Street, Mermaid Beach QLD 4218

www.echobooks.com.au

Copyright ©Milena Cifali

Creator: Cifali, Milena, Author.

Title: Mallacoota Time:the lost summer 2020

ISBN: 978-0-6488545-2-4 (Paperback)

 A catalogue record for this book is available from the National Library of Australia

Book layout and design by Peter Gamble, Canberra.

Set in Garamond Premier Pro Light Display, 12/17 and Smudgers regular.

www.echobooks.com.au

Front cover image: Milena Cifali

Back cover image: Ishak Masukor: *Space No 7*

Songs and verse are all by Milena Cifali unless otherwise noted.

Echo books web site: *https://www.echobooks.com.au/biography/mallacoota-time/*

Author's web site: *www.mallacootatime.com.au*

MALLACOOTA TIME
the lost summer 2020

Milena Cifali

ECHO BOOKS

TABLE OF CONTENTS

About the Author	ix
Acknowledgements	xi
Foreword	xiii
Preface	xv
New Year's Eve 2019	1
The Tanaka	7
Emergency	11
Homecoming	15
Journey	19
Hiatus	21
Eleven Betka Road	25
It's Too Soon	33
So Many Questions...	41
Music, my Elixir	47
Fear	51
Canberra	57
Homesickness	61
Gifts	69
Queen Corona	75
Trolley Man	83
The Oka	91

Grieving	97
The Great Pause	103
Art	107
Music	115
The Full Moon Cafe	119
The Never-Ending Chai	123
The Lost Summer	133
Friends	139
Memories	143
Moving	147
Reflections on Home	153
Menagerie	157
Remnants	163
The Red Dog	165
Julie	167
The Snake Track	173
Pilgrimage	175
Supposing	181

ABOUT THE AUTHOR

Milena Cifali, Canberra based award-winning singer, songwriter, published poet (*Love, Art, Ideas and Politics* 2020 and *Messages From The Embers, Australian Bushfire Poetry Anthology* 2020) and author, lost her home and slice of paradise in Mallacoota on New Year's Eve 2019.

Milena studied classical guitar at the ANU with Timothy Kain and Carolyn Kidd, graduating in 2000, going on to be a founding member of the Canberra Classical Guitar Society and a well respected Canberra guitar teacher and performer.

In 2011 she left Canberra and as a singer-songwriter, began touring and performing along the eastern seaboard with her partner Jim Horvath. In March 2019 Milena was invited by Canberra poet John Passant to collaborate on his published anthologies, and set about composing music for their CD *Whose Broken Is This?* which they toured with great success. In late 2019 Milena was selected as a semi-finalist in the UK international Songwriters Contest receiving a judges commendation.

Having performed to acclaim nationally at major folk festivals, Covid-19 restrictions slowed her travels. After losing her home, Milena and her partner settled in Canberra, where they currently reside, tending to the local wildlife, and performing locally. Milena is a keen photographer, birdwatcher and poet.

Acknowledgements

This book, which from a vision in my mind's eye has become a reality, has been the cumulative result of many people's energies.

Firstly, I would like to thank Peter Gamble from Echo Books for his expert layout and design of the book, and his unwavering belief in the book.

Thank you Peter, couldn't have done it without you. Also to Joce Jenkins from Echo Books for embracing my story.

My dear friend Eleni Roumeliotis, for her eagle-eyed editing, and her ever-present support. Thank you Eleni for endless late night discussions about this book.

To author and friend Peter Rodgers for reading my manuscript, providing advice and contributing the preface to this book. My sincere thanks Peter.

To author and fellow Mallacootan Jim Sakkas for his early reading of my manuscript and his contribution to the back cover of this book. Thanks Jim.

To poet Lorne Johnson, sincere thanks for the inclusion of your poem *Trolley Man* in the chapter on Joseph Cindric.

To Pamela Kinnear, thank you for the donation of the computer with which I wrote this book. It almost certainly wouldn't have happened without it.

To my son Louie Griffith for your unwavering loyalty, support and practical assistance from the moment you learnt we had lost our home, thank you, you kept me from falling apart, and also to my son Bryn Griffith for opening up his heart and home to us in Brisbane when we had nowhere else to go. Thank you, it meant so very much. I love you both.

To my mother, Maya Cifali, for her advice in the process of publishing and for unconditional lifelong support and love. To my father Guido Cifali, thank you for reading my manuscript and your invaluable advice, and for the love, understanding and life philosophies you have always provided me along my journey.

To my life partner Jim Horvath, thank you for understanding how important this book has been for healing my heart, and for putting up with my stress, and my days tucked away writing my story.

There are many people who offered special gifts and kindnesses, after we lost our home and set up a new one in Canberra: too many to mention, but know that your love and gifts have contributed to making our new house home.

To Patricia Langenakker for permission to print images and the poetry of her dear husband our cherished friend John Passant.

To Leanne Wicks, poet and dear friend, for your expert care and love of our birds, for your reading of my manuscript and advice: I raise a cup of orange and cinnamon tea to you.

To Ranjan Chadhuri for your expert proof-reading.

Special heartfelt thanks to Neville Braybrook, our friend and bushfire recovery caseworker who has been by our side every step of the way in this tumultuous journey, and without whom I may not have had the clarity of mind and heart to write this book.

Thank you all. My heart is full. *Namaste.*

FOREWORD

In writing this bushfire memoir my hope is that the bushfire ravaged communities that have suffered tremendous losses during the 'Lost Summer' of 2019-2020, can find solace and connection within its pages.

Personally, the unravelling of my own tightly-coiled emotions has been somewhat aided by the sharing of my story. It is a story that reverberates across this nation, echoing still as we take steps on our journey towards recovery... It is a story of loss—yet ultimately it is one of hope, and that is the message that I wish to share, in the sincere desire that my story can contribute to our rebuilding, both personally and nationally.

Milena Cifali

June 2020

Preface

The statistics of Australia's 2020 summer bushfires tell an awful story. Around 19 million hectares burnt, at least 34 people killed, nearly 2,800 homes destroyed, bird and animal deaths in the billions. But to truly comprehend the scale of devastation we need the personal stories behind these numbers.

That's what musician, song writer and poet, Milena Cifali, gives us in this heartfelt, illuminating and compelling book.

On New Year's Eve 2019, the little red cedar cottage in coastal Mallacoota which Milena and her partner, Jim Horvath, called home was one of the many razed. Their beloved menagerie of parrots fell victim, all of their precious musical instruments were destroyed. Milena 'cracked into a million pieces'. The world no longer made sense.

Like a bushfire, this multi-layered story swirls in unanticipated directions: devastation, numbing loss, irritation, uncertainty, hope, recovery, wonder at unexpected acts of kindness. Milena writes of returning to the 'simple yet powerful realisation: that people are kind, I am awed'.

At the heart of the story is the idea of home. Not four walls, but what they contain: music, friends, love, laughter; the gifts which amplify our lives, and which statistics can never convey.

Peter Rodgers
Prize-winning journalist and author

Adversity is a cloak that shrouds great gifts. It is up to us to cast away the cloak, revealing all that lies within.

This is the journey.

Milena Cifali

New Year's Eve 2019

Everything is gone!
Everything.

Summer 2020, a charred scarred summer that no one will ever forget...

The sun sinks on a balmy Brisbane day and the breeze wraps its cooling tendrils around us.

I've watched for hours with growing trepidation as our remote coastal hometown of Mallacoota has been threatened all day by an oncoming firestorm from Wyngan in East Gippsland, Victoria.

Photographs of Mallacoota skies turning orange, red and then black are shared on social media and the news. *Our* Mallacoota! We are far away in Brisbane, but close, so close...

Our little cedar cottage stands silently, awaiting our return. Our beautiful parrots wait too.

Blossom and Winston, magnificent Alexandrines, with plumage of rainforest green and beaks of tropical sunset red.

'I love: YOU!' calls Blossom incessantly. Winston, shy, proud Winston, beginning to trust us enough after unspoken trauma to lock eyes, or utter a squawk...

Sookie and his little wife Annie, opalescent grass parrots that I've bonded with completely. Sookie was hit by a truck and nearly died. He is my tiny Sookie, and lets me scratch him on his mane, where the feathers thicken around the neck. My little bird lion.

Romolo. Stunning creature who stops anyone in their tracks with his lacy featherwork of neon red, gold and white. A mystery bird of magnificence. They wait, all the birds, for our return, our feathered family. Leanne, our kind friend, visits each day and sings to them, while giving them seed, water, apple and corn. They know and welcome her, but it is us they wait for...

3pm. A message on my phone: it is too late to leave Mallacoota. Take shelter now.

My heart skips a beat. I call our bird friend. Ask if our evacuation plan for the birds is in order.

Our bird friend is panicking. She tells me she's leaving. I understand, desperately wondering who to call. The birds *must* leave the house. I call this person, another, a third, my panic mounting. Everyone is panicking. No one is thinking about birds, but rather their own survival.

Finally, I recall a friend who is staying home to fight the oncoming fires. Keith agrees to go and give our birds plenty of food and water and move their cages to the centre of the room away from the radiant heat of windows He turns on the sprinklers and locks the door and leaves.

The black sky above Mallacoota turning day to night. Menacing, warning of imminent catastrophe...

We learn that the fire is approaching the airport at Mallacoota, just a few kilometres south of our home. We wait. There is no celebration this New Year's Eve. Only waiting. Time stands still...

9pm. My phone rings, disturbing our silent waiting. My heart leaps. A flustered voice: our friend Donald Ashby.

'I've been for a drive, I'm still alive. My home is gone and so is yours. Sorry. Bye.'

And so is yours.

Ours! Our home is gone. Our. Home. Is Gone.

Gone.

The foundations that make one whole fall into disarray. The world no longer makes sense.

I have cracked into a million pieces.

Cannot compute. Cannot process. Unfathomable. Everything is gone!

Everything.

9.10pm, we sit in silence, my partner and I. I make a cup of tea. There will be no champagne tonight...

All is quiet on New Year's Day...

A warm, breezy Brisbane morning awaits after a fitful night of sleep, wrestling anxiety and bedsheets, ashen images playing out in my mind.

We turn on ABC News 24, and there it is: an image of our home, flattened, razed to the ground. Ash and rubble. Rubble and ash. As the day passes, that image is replayed over and over, on ABC, SBS, *A Current Affair*; it is *the* picture that has been chosen to be replayed incessantly. There is no doubt it is ours. There is no escaping.

All day these images flash before our eyes. They tell us we are not dreaming. A photo emerges on the news of a young boy, in a boat on the lake, with a mask on, under blood red skies. That is one of my guitar students. Last time I saw him he was sitting next to me, guitar in hand, laughing, with one of our lorikeets sitting on his head, his face full of delight. Now I see his face: eyes filled with trepidation, experiencing a terrifying ordeal that no child should have to endure.

On New Year's Day I write a poem. My love story with Mallacoota is finished.

Possum Requiem—Ode To Mallacoota

The phone rang.
He told us we had lost our home.
'I've been for a drive, I'm still alive.
My home is gone and so is yours.'
Engulfed in flames on New Year's Eve.
Just too hard to believe...
How do I say goodbye to our ancient tree
that held so many birds safe in its arms?
How do I say goodbye to a koala, our koala, Aristotle,
sheltered in its crook?
The birds. Our birds!
A glimpse of golden light in the Western sky
and then,
gelato colours,
softest pinks and blues,

Mallacoota hues...
fading to dark revealing glittering stars
above Mallacoota waves.
On the cool night balcony
the salt air wrapping its gentle breezes
around us, and caressing our souls...
how do I say goodbye to a night-time visit from our possum friend,
who gave us possum hugs?
Is he alive? Did he survive?
My heart beats in time with this forest and this sea.
How can it be that I must say goodbye to this paradise?
I can always buy a new toaster, a kettle, a cup, a plate,
but it's too late, too late,
to sit together on our old blue couch on our verandah,
and watch the rainbow lorikeets frolic, or Mrs Magpie sing
for her supper,
or play guitar in the morning sun
and music with friends on a full moon night.
Wherever I may roam I may create a new home:
but this sense of place has gone.
This was our Mallacoota magic.
How tragic.

The Tanaka

A sense of place

The birds. The birds. *The birds*. Every hour of every day my mind settles, but tries not to settle, on our beautiful bird family that died trapped in their cages, engulfed in flames. We weren't there to protect them! Vile, horrific, tragic, needless! But then no one thinks their home will burn down.

Minutes become hours, days become weeks...

Caught in a surreal kind of sleep-walking perpetual numbness, mixed with sharp twinges of anxiety and irritability. Occasionally I cry. In the supermarket, or swimming laps. Always at the most inopportune times... I just want to go home. But I can't.

Brisbane becomes our limbo lounge as we await a safe time to return south. But to where? To what? Uncertainty looms. Here, at least we see clear blue skies, hearing only of smoking, choking skies further south.

Here it is breezy, there are palm trees, ibises, lizards and greenery. One can imagine that all is well.

Our days pass in a daze, numbly eating ice-cream, riding a ferry on the river, vacantly taking in the view, trying not to think too hard. We meet friends in Brisbane. They give us things. A red teapot. A ceramic bird. A cushion. Clothes. A care package for the bathroom. So many things, but nowhere to put them—still, I am grateful for the kindnesses people demonstrate to us.

I'm interviewed by the BBC on New Year's Eve. Listening back, I'm amazed at how in control and calm I sound.

I think it's shock. I start to develop a stutter. My mouth feels dry and I have trouble forming words. We meet friends for lunch and I have a tight feeling in my chest the whole time, feeling that I must smile, must make conversation, must not stutter. The pressure is intense.

My mind wanders compulsively over every corner of our cedar cottage in Mallacoota. Every surface, each shelf, every room. I write lists of what I've lost. Everyday I remember something new.

My mother's first stuffed toy. A photo of me when I was three. My grandmother's Persian carpet of midnight blue and palest pink which my ancestors walked on. In its life, it travelled from Alexandria, Egypt, to Alice Springs, Sydney to Canberra, and ultimately to Mallacoota. Boxes and boxes of my life's work of guitar compositions, many meticulously hand-written. I'm angry! I've left them there, to burn! How will I remember them? I can't! Books, an entire library of them, all well-thumbed and contributing to the person I am today. All turned to ash. Photograph albums. Every day there is a new flash of realisation, of something else that is gone.

People meet us, ask where we are from, and upon hearing 'Mallacoota' they ask if we were okay in the fires. *No. Our home burnt down.*

Did you have insurance? they ask.

I'm infuriated. How dare they? They don't ask 'are you ok' or 'do you need anything?' or 'I'm sorry'...

I feel like they have ripped my bag open and are searching its contents.

Yes. We do have insurance, but it won't bring back my little mouse, made of felt, in a tiny embroidered dress, with her delicate whiskers, holding a miniature basket with a baby mouse in it. When I was ten years old,

I went to watch Trevor White and Jon English performing in *Jesus Christ Superstar* at a beautiful art deco theatre in Sydney. I was bursting with excitement. Before the show, we went to The Rocks and my mother bought me my little mouse. My mouse represented the sheer joy and excitement of that experience in my childhood. It was one of my most treasured possessions.

Yes! I have insurance! But it won't bring me back my little mouse! I feel like screaming at them.

They won't understand so I say nothing, but feel my anger rising...

I'm at a Turkish store and the Iraqi man at the counter asks how we are, where we are from.

'Mallacoota, our home burnt down on New Year's Eve.'

'Oh no!' he says. 'Have anything you want! My shop is yours! Take what you need!'

'No, no we are okay' I say.

'Please, please! Take something!' he says.

I see a small Turkish coffee pot, made of copper. I've never been without one in my life.

My parents were born in Alexandria, Egypt and I grew up watching my grandmother making coffee in a little *'tanaka'*.

'I would love this *tanaka*,' I say.

'Of course! Of course!' says our Iraqi friend.

I leave, without a kitchen, without a stove, and without a Turkish coffee cup, but with my *tanaka*, feeling ever so slightly more at home again.

EMERGENCY

*In an instant,
life has changed*

My partner Jim suffered a stroke four weeks before our home burnt down.

We had been practising music, and as day faded to night he stood up and said, 'I can't see. I've lost my vision in one eye. It's all gone black.'

My mouth went dry and my pulse quickened. I told him I'd call a doctor.

'I'll be alright, don't call a doctor!' he said.

'No, you're not alright. You can't see. I'm calling a doctor.'

This went on for a couple of minutes. Finally, I called the town doctor and told him my partner had lost his vision suddenly.

'It is a medical emergency. You must call an ambulance.'

An ambulance officer, then a second and a third arrived at the door within minutes. Efficient, calm, professional, leaving no doubt in my mind that this indeed was a medical emergency.

We are in an ambulance, winding out of Mallacoota on the dark twenty-three kilometre stretch of road that leads to the highway. Left to Melbourne, right to Sydney.

In an instant, life has changed. Ten minutes ago we'd been playing music, about to eat dinner. Now we are racing to Bega Hospital, dodging wallabies in an ambulance on the dark road.

My mouth tastes metallic and dry. My stomach is churning. My palms are sweaty.

Why has my partner lost his vision?

1am: Bega Hospital. Bright lights, white walls, questions and more questions.

Why are you here? What is your name? Date of birth? What day of the week is it?

Wheeled away at 2am for a CAT scan. The carotid artery is critically narrowed. There is not enough blood flowing to the brain.

Surgery on the carotid artery is in order. This is a life-threatening condition. My partner must be transferred to Canberra Hospital immediately for surgery.

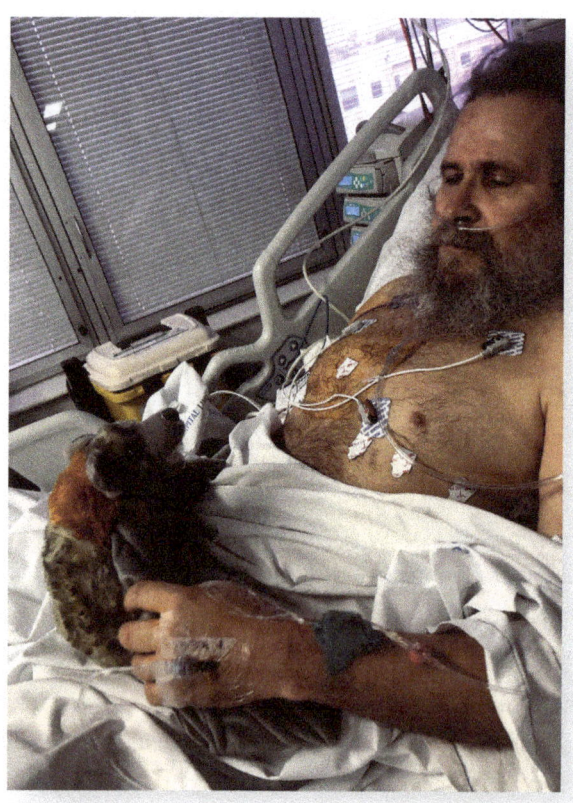

3am: Another ambulance and a three-hour trip over the dark and winding Brown Mountain road to Canberra. We are transferred to an upstairs ward in the stroke unit. Mercifully, at 4am, I am given a recliner, a blanket and earplugs, allowing an hour or two of sleep...

8am: my partner is wheeled in for surgery, a three to four hour operation, I'm informed.

It has been explained to us that this particular surgery, a carotid endarterectomy, is very risky: four in one hundred suffer a stroke, one in a hundred a heart attack, and there is a high risk of waking with slurred speech due to damage to the nerves around the jaw and neck.

The other option, not undergoing the surgery, is worse: one in four suffer a full blown, incapacitating stroke within the first forty-eight hours after suffering a minor stroke.

The decision is clear. We must proceed.

I wait and wait. Again, with anxiety gnawing quietly at my insides.

Three hours become four, five become six... After seven hours, I am finally called to the Intensive Care Unit where I can see Jim.

I am sitting by his bed under the bright lights. His gown is hospital blue and his sheets and pillow are white. Why are the sheets in hospitals and hotels always so impossibly white? There are tubes everywhere. Machines beeping. Suddenly I see red splotches, like watercolour poppies, spreading on the immaculate white pillow. The red blooms are multiplying rapidly. I then see blood spurting from Jim's neck.

I feel faint. Not wanting to alarm him, I stand up and walk to the nearest nurse, out of earshot. I tell her my partner is bleeding from the neck. All at once, there are one, two, then three nurses attending to the bleeding. Then a doctor arrives. For the next few minutes I stand back, as the alarming situation is rectified. I am shaken, but grateful that once again the pillow is white.

ICU becomes our home for a week. I rarely leave Jim's side and sleep fitfully on a recliner near his bed.

We came to Canberra with nothing, apart from the clothes on our backs, my handbag and telephone. I have no car, toothbrush, or fresh clothes.

Our friends kindly bring plastic bags from Big W and K-Mart with clothes they have chosen for me.

They bring toiletries. They bring hampers of food. *People are kind.*

I am stressed, worrying endlessly about whether to cancel gigs, whether Jim will be able to drive, whether we will go to Brisbane for a Christmas family reunion, whether Jim will be capable of playing bass or learning new music. I am so stressed.

We receive visits from the neuropsychologist, and the Occupational Health Team, and the Vascular Surgeon.

Finally the day arrives. We can go home.

Homecoming

I stretch and sigh.
I'm home ...

Home. What is home?
 The place where one lives, eats and sleeps. The place where one returns to, with relief, after time spent away.

Where one keeps one's things. *Things.* One's books, clothes. Knives, forks. Photograph albums. Jewellery. One's own pillow. A feather found on the ground, placed carefully in a vase. Letters kept over the years, in a box in the cupboard. Diaries, recording memories and emotions otherwise clouded by time. Jars of lentils and rice

on the kitchen bench. Favourite flavours of tea in red canisters, to match one's red couch, and red Turkish lampshades. A place where one can sit on the hand-painted Chinese stool that has been lovingly restored and play one's guitar of choice: perhaps the handmade concert guitar that sounds like a fine malt whiskey, or perhaps the bright treble steel string guitar inlaid with a dragon made of mother of pearl that sounds like a crisp dry white, or perhaps the cedar top Spanish Alhambra that sounds like a mellow woody red...

Home: *homecoming*. The feeling of relief and comfort when one has been away for too long.

I turn the key in the front door. There is a little jiggle, just so, that is required to allow the key to turn and unlock the door. There is a smell, a homely scent, that whispers *welcome*...

I am home. I let out a sigh. I can cook soup. With *my* wooden spoon. I know its handle, the way it feels in my hand, so well. The home fills with the smell of homemade soup.

And after dinner, on our red couch, the sublime feeling of falling into our own bed, with peacock green sheets and pillows, not hospital white. I lie in bed and luxuriate in the peace, listening to the Mallacoota waves as they lull me to sleep on my own pillow...

Mallacoota Time

There's an ache in my bones, I want to go home
Been away for so long, I've sung every song
Turning off the highway, pull into the driveway,
unlock the door, put the kettle on
It's time to unwind,
'cause haven't you heard, I'm doing fine
I'm on Mallacoota Time

Sit on the verandah feel the ocean breeze in my face
I belong in this place
listening to the ocean hum, soaking up the gentle sun
everything unwinding at the pace that it should

I'm feeling good
'cause haven't you heard I'm doing fine
I'm on Mallacoota Time...

Take me back to the shoreline...
Pelicans floating out on the lake
Sea eagles gliding on the breeze
kookaburra laughs in the old gum tree
Koala drops by to say hello
Surely it's not time to go
'cause haven't you heard I'm doing fine
I'm on Mallacoota Time....

JOURNEY

The sky is thick with smoke ...

It is hot. Thirty-seven degrees on Tuesday. Thirty-eight on Wednesday. Forty-one on Thursday. It is dry. Most of the country is in drought. Dams are drying up. Sheep and cattle are dying. Australia is parched. Trees are suffering. Our garden is yellowing...

The Country Fire Authority (CFA) comes to Mallacoota to give a talk to prepare the community in the event of a bushfire. They explain that this year's fires have been unprecedented. The flames have been hotter, higher, faster, more ferocious. The ground is tinder dry. They explain that from Cann River, about seventy kilometres away, a fire will potentially travel that distance in one hour. Mallacoota only has one road in and out. The community must be prepared. The warning is loud and clear. Leave early. Do not defend your home alone. If it is too late to leave, remain indoors. Wear wool, leather boots, long pants.

Radiant heat will kill you before the fire does. You will perish from smoke inhalation before the flames even arrive. Stay indoors. Do not attempt to leave your home until the fire-front has passed.

'We have a cedar cottage, and my partner has had a stroke. What should we do?' I ask.

'Get the hell out,' is the response I am given. A twinge of anxiety.

Jim has another vision loss episode, a brief flash of darkness. There is that twinge of anxiety, again.

The doctor says it's normal. Bits of plaque breaking away and hitting the back of the eye, or the brain. I don't know what normal is anymore.

We make plans to go to Brisbane for Christmas. We will reunite with my family, and we also have a show booked at Doo-Bop Jazz Lounge in Brisbane city. We are excited to be performing there, a week after James Morrison and a week before The Black Sorrows.

I am relieved that Jim has been given clearance to drive, as I haven't driven for six years, although I am prepared to do so if needed. Finally, we decide to drive the big bus, our Oka, to Brisbane, taking it slowly. We are forced to cancel gigs along the way at Mollymook and Sussex Inlet, North of Batemans Bay as that section of the South Coast is on fire.

The sky is thick with smoke as we head towards Canberra via Cooma, driving through dying landscape. There is a faded yellow look to everything.

Heading along the highway towards Sydney, the sky begins to glow orange and then red. The heat is stifling. Near Bargo the highway closes. We hear helicopters and see black smoke billowing nearby. I make a snap decision. We head out to the coast towards Wollongong.

Winding into Wollongong the sky turns blue and we can breathe again. We are looking forward to our ten days away in Brisbane over Christmas before returning home...

HIATUS

... the cool breezes ... caress my soul

We have been in Brisbane almost a month. My son Bryn has opened his door to us and made us feel welcome.

'Here's your bed, here's the fridge, stay as long as you need.'

We haven't seen our place in Mallacoota yet since it was destroyed, apart from in photos. It looks like a bomb site. It still doesn't feel real. I feel like a friend has died but I've not been able to see the body.

I don't feel like eating and have trouble swallowing food. All I want to eat is ice-cream, and perhaps a juicy Queensland mango. I'm exhausted all the time. I fall asleep early and wake as the sun is rising. I have no energy to do anything.

Mallacoota has been in lockdown. People have been trapped there, the roads are closed, due to safety issues such as burning trees falling on the roads. Tourists are unable to leave. There is limited fuel, no power, food shortages. And a pub with no beer. The navy sends in two ships to evacuate tourists out of Mallacoota to Melbourne. News footage emerges of dusty, tired, shell-shocked people in single file queueing to board the ships. Fire refugees.

One hundred and forty homes in Mallacoota have been destroyed.

Today I wake depressed. I lie on the mattress staring at the ceiling, feeling disconnected from my body. I feel strangely invisible, as though I am made of ash...

I write:

> My home is a pile of ash but I will rebuild.
> The bush is a pile of ash but it will regenerate.
> My emotions are a pile of ash but they will rearrange.
> My garden is a pile of ash but I will replant.
> My thoughts are made of ash but I will rethink.
> My heart is a pile of ash but it will reform.
> My soul is made of ash but it will rebirth.
> I am made of ash but I will return. From the rubble will rise new thoughts, new life.
> It will take a long time, but I will be alright
> after this dark ash night.
> Rain will wash away the ash wash away the hurt wash away the loss.
> Wash away.
> I will begin anew...

Today, we are driving to Lismore to perform at The Dusty Attic. This is a show we had booked months ago, and we decide not to cancel it. I'm unsure of how I will be able to perform given my fragile emotional state, but we decide we will do our best. The show must go on.

We have a friend in Lismore, Deb Mills, who has organised a crowd to come and support us.

I arrive in Lismore, hot, sweaty and sleepy. We find a cool grassy knoll near the river, under a tree, and I crawl into the back of the Oka, onto our bed, open all the windows and allow the cool cross-breezes to caress my soul.

I wonder at the irony of it: the fire destroyed our home, our birds, our instruments, everything in it. But we still have an Oka, one bass, one guitar, three folders of songs, a backpack of clothes, and a PA. We have all that is required to travel to and perform a show. And six lorikeets and three budgerigars. Yes, some of our little bird family travelled with us to Brisbane, and remain with us still.

The exact opposite happened to a musician friend of ours from Candelo, the small NSW township that was ravaged by fires also. The fire missed his home, which remained intact, but devoured his van, along with his musical instruments, PA and music. Life is strange.

So, here we are by the river in Lismore gearing up to perform our first show since our home burnt down.

We are setting up at The Dusty Attic. People are beginning to arrive. I have never had to perform in this situation. A post-fire performance. This is a first for me. The lights dim, the audience is seated. There is an expectant hush.

I begin with Mallacoota Time. *'There's an ache in my bones. I want to go home...'*

I read my poem about saying goodbye to Mallacoota. I sing this song, that song, I tell stories. When I speak to the audience I feel nervous.

My voice wavers with emotion. But when I sing, it's different. I'm here. Grounded. Anchored. Music does that. It's like coming home...

Eleven Betka Road

Birds! So many birds!

As soon as I approached the door of the cedar cottage in Mallacoota seven years ago, I knew I was home. We had been travelling for a year or so after renting out my house in Canberra, after which time I had decided to sell it and was considering buying something along the coast.

Mallacoota was breathtakingly beautiful. Pristine lakes and beaches. Pelicans, koalas and kangaroos, and a musically and artistically-inclined community. A remote location, cheap real estate, and exactly halfway between Melbourne and Sydney.

We literally stumbled upon this little cottage, 11 Betka Road. What a lovely number. *Eleven*.

A five minute walk to the beach. From the front verandah, one could hear the waves. I'd always dreamt of the magic of being lulled to sleep by the sound of waves from my own home. The little cottage was bright and airy, with high timber ceilings and a loft. Within a month we had moved in.

We went couch shopping in Melbourne and bought a red leather couch. That set the theme. Red Turkish beaded lamps, a red teapot. Red coffee machine. We hung our artworks on our walls. Slowly, as one does, we acquired things. Cushions, rugs, a red enamel jug. I unpacked treasures from my trip to Europe with my sons Bryn and Louie in 2003. Miniature guitars made of wood and intricate silver, Tuscan pottery jugs and saucers in sunshine and sea colours, Chinese *cloisonne* gold and brilliant turquoise pots with a sapphire blue enamel glaze inside each pot, designed like Babushka dolls to stack inside each other... a tiny exquisite magnifying glass with silver handle and a navy blue tassel, purchased at a flea market in Lausanne, Switzerland, my birthplace.

Lovingly unwrapping treasures my grandmother Aimee had left to me: a brass crocodile nutcracker, a miniature silver Aladdin's lamp, small silver dishes from Alexandria, an engraved silver chest, with a handwritten note from her, and a worn leather one with an antique coin collection... My initialled Florentine jewellery box, made of Italian embossed leather, purchased at a jewellery boutique on the famous Ponte Vecchio spanning the Arno River and containing a gold mosaic cross, my reward for climbing the hundreds of spiralling stairs to the roof of the Vatican in Rome. Two gold pendants on a gold chain gifted to me when I was newborn, and an Italian silver bracelet with my name *Milena* engraved on it and given to me by my grandmother in Rome when I was a child. Opening the lid of my jewellery box meant diving back into my history, revisiting treasured objects speaking to me of cherished moments in my life...

We slept in the loft in the first few years, watching the stars, the moon rise, and then the sunrise... woken early by the chattering birds.

Birds. So many birds! We were treated to an endless parade, all day, every day. They came in turn: first the King Parrots resplendent in green and red, then the Rosellas, royal red and indigo blue, followed by Mrs and Mr Magpie in their dinner suits of black and white, quickly followed by the unruly and boisterous Lorikeets, all dressed in rainbow suits, chattering endlessly about their latest pursuits. There were always the Wonga Pigeons, fat, lazy, grey and white, rarely flying, happy to sun-bake and coo endlessly, grazing on food that only they knew about... in the golden afternoon the Galahs would arrive, in groups of two or three, pink, grey, cheeky. Overhead, the call of Black Cockatoos on their way elsewhere...

The kookaburras were our special friends. A week or two after we arrived in Mallacoota, I was on the back verandah calling our magpies in: 'Maggie!' when suddenly there appeared before me a very beautiful kookaburra who looked me straight in the eye with her warm, long-lashed brown ones, and allowed me to feed her by hand.

She was named *Mama Kooka* and promptly became my best friend. She would come to sit and chat, recount her woes. One day, she arrived at our place as usual, but kept flying up into the big gum tree in our backyard insistently wanting to show us something. What was it? It was a fledgling kookaburra, her baby. That baby was Elmo, and he became my partner's best friend. They too shared an amazing bond, and Elmo would come when called and land on Jim's arm.

Then there was Bung Eye. Bung Eye was a one-eyed currawong that appeared one day out of nowhere. He was in a sorry state and we took a liking to him and began feeding him. He would wait at the window for us. One day, he flew away with his tribe, to the high country for the summer months. We thought that was the end of it, but a year later, the following winter, we arrived home one day to find Bung Eye sitting on our back verandah.

This same thing happened three winters running. One day we returned home to find that Bung Eye had built a nest, and had two hatchlings of her own. Our boy Bung Eye had become a mother and was in fact a 'she'.

In the late afternoon, our garden would take on a golden green hue so exquisite that I would sit entranced, just to enter into that light and feel the weight of its beauty; it was a light that I have never encountered elsewhere before or since...

In our front garden we attracted tiny little birds, fire tails, with seeds which we put out each day in the bird feeders hanging from trees.

Birds were all around us, a part of our daily lives and routines. Before even partaking of our morning coffee, our own birds required our care and attention first. They were all rescue birds and none would have survived in the wild. We loved all our birds dearly. Each bird, wild or otherwise, had its own unique character and habits. Over the years we came to know and love their idiosyncrasies.

The birds made our house home as much as our artworks, couches, friends, or a pot of soup cooking on the stove...

I pay homage to our feathered friends.

Amongst the wildlife surrounding us in Mallacoota was also a possum family.

One of the possums took a liking to Jim. When we would return home from a musical tour, he would hear the Oka arriving in the driveway and come bounding towards us just as a puppy would. He would then stand upright and hug Jim around his legs. A homecoming welcome.

Then there was Aristotle. Aristotle was an old and wise koala. In Aboriginal culture the koala is associated with wisdom. Aristotle would come and go, wandering from tree to tree in our vicinity. One of those trees was directly outside our home. He would announce his arrival with loud snorting. The first time I heard that sound I thought there was a wild pig in our tree.

To fall asleep in our own bed, to the sound of the waves, with Aristotle snorting outside is something I will always associate with Mallacoota...

Apart from wild birds, koalas and possums, we had visits from a very large goanna who adopted one of our trees for a few days, ruffling a few feathers in the process.

There were also mornings when we would wake to big grey kangaroos sitting in our backyard, staring at us as if to say, 'What are you doing here?'

At the end of the fire season, which ran from early August 2019 through to end of February 2020, and was truly unprecedented in its frequency and severity along the Eastern seaboard, 18.6 million hectares of bushland had been destroyed, and an estimated two billion animals had perished. These included birds, bats, amphibians, insects, reptiles and mammals. Many endangered species had been pushed to the brink of extinction. The after-effects of the fire season devastated existing wildlife and included starvation, attacks from predators such as feral cats and foxes and lack of adequate shelter. The loss of approximately eight thousand koalas has left the Australian icon vulnerable to extinction.

Smoke had drifted across the South Pacific to New Zealand, Argentina, Chile, Uruguay and Brazil. In the cities of Sydney, Melbourne and Canberra smoke reached hazardous levels. On the first of January 2020 in Canberra the Air Quality Index was measured at more than twenty-three times hazardous levels.

There were constant evacuations along the eastern seaboard, skies were an ominous mix of yellow, red and even grey most days, and a blue sky had become a rarity.

This was a fire season like no other, and is now referred to colloquially as *The Lost Summer...*

I know I'm blessed. I am merely grieving the loss of years of musical compositions, music, recordings, my writing, my artwork, family treasures. My sense of place. *Home.*

But on a much deeper level I am suffering from *solastalgia*, a form of emotional and existential distress caused by environmental change. Philosopher Glenn Albrecht introduced the term in 2005, a combination of the Greek root *'algia'* meaning 'pain' and the Latin word *'solacium'* (comfort).

Solastalgia is when your endemic sense of place is being violated.
Glenn Albrecht.

I mourn not only our cedar cottage at 11 Betka, but the loss of trees, birds, ants, butterflies, koalas, echidnas, lizards, bees, frogs, forests, oceans, and ultimately the fragile ecosystem hanging by an ever so delicate thread...

It's Too Soon

I sit in stunned silence ...

Decisions. When one has suffered trauma, decision-making can become challenging.

Tea or coffee a friend asks. My mind goes into mild panic. I must make a choice and it feels difficult.

People keep asking us, apart from whether we have insurance:

So, will you rebuild?

I can't even choose between tea and coffee, let alone when, how, where and if we will rebuild. These are enormous life decisions. It is not like asking *will you brush your teeth?*

The fact that people seem intent on asking us if we will rebuild produces anxiety followed by irritability.

I want to snap, 'How can I possibly answer that!' but instead I answer, 'It's too soon.'

Jim has a cancerous growth spreading fast under his left eye, very close to the tear duct. He is scheduled for surgery in Canberra to remove it. I am juggling appointments with optometrists, vascular surgery follow-ups, ultrasounds and plastic surgery all from Brisbane, and at the same time I'm expected to be dealing with insurance companies, writing emails, and getting ready to find a rental property in Canberra. It's all overwhelming. Fortunately my son Louie in Canberra is very proactive in dealing with this side of things on our behalf, as my brain is overloaded and just can't cope with any of this at the moment.

Another function that is sometimes affected after experiencing trauma is memory. I have trouble recalling if I have made an appointment, whether I wrote it down and who I still need to contact.

I am keeping a close watch on the *Fires Near Me* App to ascertain when and if it will be safe to travel to Canberra. I keep hearing about smoke filled skies and watching new fires appear, and out of control ones getting bigger and fiercer. The fires this season are hungry monsters, devouring everything in their path.

My nerves feel shot to pieces. I see that there will be a few days of rain along the North Coast, and begin planning our return journey from Brisbane to Canberra.

On the 19th January, 2020, twenty days after our home burnt down, and a month after arriving in Brisbane, we finally pack the Oka and head South.

I am dreading heading South. All I see and hear about are fires and drought. We have nowhere to live in Canberra but my son has organized a motel for us for two weeks.

We stop at The Entrance near Sydney for two nights at an apartment complex where accommodation has been offered to people who have lost their homes in the bushfires. Our apartment is on the seventh floor. We arrive and there is a box of chocolates, a bottle of wine, and a hand written note which reads:

> 'We are so sorry about your loss. Please enjoy these items compliments of this hotel. Welcome Home.'

I read the note three times. It makes me cry. I am not home. But people mean kindness...

Our friend, luthier Peter Villaume arrives at The Entrance to meet us with four handmade concert guitars. My beauty was lovingly and expertly hand-crafted by Peter Villaume, and I purchased it from him at the Newcastle Guitar Festival many years ago. It had developed beautifully with age, and was acquiring the most sublime earthy tone, before being engulfed in flames in Mallacoota.

Peter gives me a hug and we open up the four cases. It is like meeting four new people, each with her own accent, hair colour and soul.

I play the first, a blonde beauty, sharp, trill, extroverted. I acquaint myself with the second, a cedar guitar with wooden tones, and a loud disposition. The third guitar is immediately captivating. A blonde with warmth, balanced with a restrained rounded beauty in tone. The fourth guitar is not for me. Our chemistry doesn't click.

Finally I say, 'Peter. It's this one. The third guitar.'

He is glad I have chosen this one, it is the one, he says, that he would have chosen for me.

'How much will it set me back?'

'You can have it,' he says matter-of-factly.

'No, no. I'll pay it off, send you the money.'

'It's yours. Don't argue. I want you to have it. It's yours.'

I sit in stunned silence with my new guitar. It is not my old cedar beauty of delicious whiskey tones. I must let that go... but it's my new, blonde, warm and witty guitar, and we will grow to like each other very much.

I am touched by this kindness...

We leave The Entrance, new blonde guitar—whom I have named *Sydney*—in tow.

Between the New South Wales towns of Mittagong and Goulburn we hit the epicentre of two enormous dust-storms.

I see scraggly sheep, cracked earth, yellow skies. Spindly dying trees. Empty creeks.

The wind howls through our windows, forty-three degrees, drying my nostrils. We sip water that has turned hot in our bus, dust stinging our eyes. I write:

> Dead bleak ashened blackened
> Like the corners of my heart
> Burning winds
> Furnace driven
> Dust bowl landscapes shrouded in dust storm skies
> The smell of acrid smoke choking, obliterating horizons.
> Mid-summer flowers fading, tempers flaring, passions jading.
> Opaque memories of our lush land
> now eroded, starved, parched.
> Scraggly magpies screaming panting thirsty
> beaks begging, begging.
> Monstrous fire clouds form above
> Hungry monsters at our heads
> Fire refugees snatching sleep in unmade hotel beds, or wherever they can lay their heads.
> Fright! Flight! Fight!
> When will peace return again, and then, even if it does,
> Will we await the next round, never again safe and sound?
> We have lost our home
> and may rebuild again.
> but somehow, things will never be the same.

We arrive in Canberra, wilted, covered in dust.

We go to collect the hire car my son has arranged for us, only to be told we can't collect it as there is a fire out of control near the airport where the hire car is. We are asked to come back tomorrow. Driving over the bridge I see plumes of black smoke across the horizon.

What have we arrived to?

We learn that we have missed a hailstorm by one day, with hailstones the size of golf balls.

Thousands of cars including my son's station wagon have been written off and buildings around Canberra damaged.

Our first night in Canberra is spent in a motel room on crisp white sheets and pillows.

The following days are heatwave days, so hot and dry. The air-conditioned room helps us forget, and when we open the door to exit, we are slapped rudely in the face by the abrupt heat.

Our motel room becomes our refuge from the heat. We lie in refrigerated air on the white sheets, staring at the white ceiling, drinking tea from white cups.

We are tired and stressed. We argue a lot, over petty nothings. We are together all the time in close quarters and the stress has put a strain on our relationship.

Jim seems grumpy most of the time, and restless. Communication is difficult. I feel misunderstood. I worry: is it the stroke causing this irritability and confusion in Jim or the trauma from the house burning down? Or the medication he is on? Perhaps it's a combination of all three.

It's a complex and interwoven puzzle to piece together...

The grass is dead, there are few birds. There is an out of control bushfire to the South of Canberra in Namadgi National Park. Over the next two days it creeps menacingly toward Canberra's southern outskirts. We drive to the top of Red Hill and photograph flames shooting off the Brindabella Mountains.

A state of emergency is declared. Smoke fills our lungs.

During this time we are searching for a place to rent. Open homes are challenging. With forty or so others we are assigned a short ten minutes to assess each house, not having the opportunity to get a realistic feeling of the home, hampered by the presence of the crowd. We leave feeling hot and stressed.

Fortunately, we manage to arrange a private inspection of a home in Belconnen, in Canberra's Northwest, in Holt. My son writes an application letter on our behalf.

The house is large and airy, and feels peaceful. As we leave I feel somehow that I know the house. It feels very familiar.

We learn ten days or so later that we have been successful in our application.

Holt is framed by horse paddocks and bushland looking out to the Brindabella Ranges where the fire is still raging. I have visions of the smoke and flames, now so close, leaping across the dry grass paddocks straight to Holt, devouring what will be our new home. Not again, I think. Not again.

During this smoke-filled and extremely dry summer, we have begun going regularly to the top of Red Hill Nature Reserve. There we have found a mob of hungry and dishevelled looking magpies. Magpies normally live in small, highly territorial family groups. These magpies are different. They have banded together in a group of thirty or so. Some have broken beaks, some have misshapen legs, some are limping, all are thirsty and starving. These are vagabond magpies. Homeless magpies. We bring a large metal bowl and fill it each day with cool fresh water. They drink and drink, relieved at last. We bring food, once a day. As soon as we exit our car, they arrive, descending upon us, screaming, begging for food. As the days pass, we begin to recognize them individually. There is Beaky, with her broken beak, and Leggy who looks as though his legs have been dipped in concrete.

These are the times where we feel togetherness, with each other and with nature. We are content, being up here, closer to the clouds and birds, doing our part to help nature survive through these intensely challenging times...

So Many Questions

'How are you doing?'

It is late January in Canberra. A friend tells me that the ABC program *Q&A* is hosting their next show from Queanbeyan, NSW, just out of Canberra, and the topic will be the bushfire crisis. I decide to apply to be a part of the audience and perhaps have a chance to ask a question to the panel.

To my surprise, I am contacted a day later to say I have been successful. They intend to air my question second on the show.

As we leave our motel to drive to Queanbeyan, visibility is poor over the road, the air so thick with smoke that I feel claustrophobic. I see small birds flying erratically, trying desperately to escape the smoke, their tiny lungs struggling to filter it out.

As we arrive at The Q, where the program will be televised, a crowd has gathered outside the building in the smoky twighlight, holding placards and flags bearing the *Xtinction Rebellion* logo. Against the smoky sunset backdrop there is a powerful sense of presence about the group.

I file to enter the theatre and am briefed about where to sit and when to ask my question.

The show was to air from Bega, but the town was ordered to evacuate due to the fires, so a lot of the audience had travelled through thick smoke from the South Coast to be present.

On the panel are Kristy McBain, mayor of Bega; Michael Mann, Professor of Atmospheric Science at Penn State University; Jim Molan, Senator for NSW; Cheryl McCarthy, Far South Coast Director, Surf Lifesaving NSW; Victor Steffensen, Indigenous fire practitioner; and Andrew Constance, member for Bega.

The audience is ushered to their seats, lights are dimmed and directed at the stage.

There is a sense of urgency in the room. People have come wanting answers to what has been a horrifically traumatic summer for all involved.

The first question is put to the panel by Graeme Freedman:

'Hi. I'm from Cobargo. We lost everything. We lost our house. Currently floating between Canberra and Cobargo. Two neighbours died, two came very close. Our community is really struggling with insurance, clean-up, fencing, uncertainty of financial assistance, on top of the emotional trauma of the fire itself and of individual personal loss. For our own health, we need—the community, and us—need to get on with our lives, though, and that's a big issue. The question really is how can you, the panel, and the government ensure that we can get the help we need and not have government agencies intruding in our lives via various forms and pressure and all of the different bureaucracy that we're having to run through at the moment?'

The panelists address the issue and then I hear my name called. I stand, collected, determined to be heard. I want to speak for the people and provide a voice for the wildlife. I want answers:

'Hi, I'm Milena. With my partner Jim here, we lost our home in Mallacoota on New Year's Eve and we've been effectively homeless since then. We're in Canberra now searching for a home. We're musicians. We've lost all our instruments and our beloved pets and we've actually been unable to return to Mallacoota at this point to set eyes on the damage.

My partner's had some medical issues which have prevented us from travelling because it's been too stressful.

In NSW alone, the bushfires have destroyed more than two thousand homes, twenty-five people have been killed and two billion wildlife have perished, if not more.

What strategies are now being formulated by the government to help those of us left homeless, our precious wildlife, and what strategies are being implemented to save us all from a national disaster of this magnitude in the future?

Thank you'.

I am surprised at how clear and loud my voice sounds, at how anchored I feel.

And I hear Hamish Macdonald, the new host of *Q&A*, ask:

'Before we get an answer to that, how are you doing?'

How are you doing? Music to my ears. Such a simple sentence, made of four simple words. How. Are. You. Doing?

And so much more sensitive and caring a question than: *Do. You. Have. Insurance?*

I reply, as best I can, as at times I really don't know how I am doing...

'It's all very surreal, because we haven't been able to get back to Mallacoota to actually take stock. We first saw an image of our home—of what was left of it, the rubble—on *ABC News* on New Year's Day. That is a very strange thing to absorb I think.

If we were with our community and all doing this together, it would be easier for us. But who knows? Perhaps it's easier being at a distance and having time to process it in different ways. But we're getting there, practically and slowly.'

Hamish Macdonald: 'Good, good to hear it.'

'Yeah. Thank you.'

Words and ideas are tossed around, skimmed like stones, the surface of my question is barely scratched. The audience calls out vindictively from time to time to panellists. There is a lot of anger in the room.

The final question of the evening is such a poignant one that it makes my tears well. Sam Wagstaff asks:

'In recent months we've seen and felt and breathed extremes in fire, smoke, heat, hail, dust and drought, all right here, or just down the road. If this is the new normal, do you think my two year old son and nine month old daughter can still share the same healthy carefree childhood that I had?'

A pertinent question indeed. My heart is heavy for the children.

So I went to Queanbeyan and asked a question to a panel of six and an audience of one hundred.

That's what I thought happened. I forgot that this was national television!

The following day, my partner and I are at a shopping mall, wandering around, buying coffee.

I am approached by a lady who grabs my hand: 'I saw you on *Q&A* last night. Well done! You were great!'

Two minutes later, a couple approaches: 'Great job on *Q&A* last night!'

This goes on all day and the following few days. Also, friends are messaging us to say that they saw Jim and me on television. They say my question was well formulated and delivered, and that it had been a compelling episode.

At *Q&A*, seated next to us in the audience, is a lady and her friend. At the end of the show, she says she has a box of percussion instruments that she feels moved to give to us. She says it's not much but she would love us to have it. I give her our number and email address.

Eight weeks later, a box arrives at our door. I have no idea who it's from or what it is. I open the box and find it filled, to my utmost delight, with an assortment of beautiful percussion instruments: a hand-painted maraca, a small green egg shaker, an African seed pod shaker, a thumb piano, some bells, a guiro, and a pair of exquisitely-crafted clapping sticks, made of mulga wood, from Central Australia, where my sons were born. The clapping sticks feel smooth and heavy in my hands. I tap them together. Their tone is ceramic and clear and I am transported to the Red Centre.

To the lady from *Q&A*, thank you so much. I have no idea who you are, but your kindness has touched me deeply.

I have received an email from *Q & A*. A woman in Port Macquarie wants to contact us to donate some instruments. Her name is Nickolina Rivers. *What a lovely melodic name*, I think.

She says she has a steel string guitar and a double bass that she feels moved to donate, and a violin.

We speak on the phone and I tell her that Jim played violin when he was a child, and that learning pathways affected by the stroke could perhaps be enhanced by learning the violin again. We arrange to meet halfway, in Newcastle, in two weeks' time.

We meet in a sunny car park and Nickolina introduces the instruments one by one, as though we are meeting new friends.

We chat a while, and then part ways. We decide to take the opportunity to dine over the water in Newcastle as the sun sets on the harbour. We then drive back to Canberra with our new friends—a guitar, a bass and a violin—arriving at 2am, tired but with a heart full of gratitude...

Constantly amazed at the kindness people demonstrate...

Music, My Elixir

...the guitar ...it's part of me.

Music, always music. Since I was old enough to remember, music was a part of my existence. My mother says I sang before I spoke.

I came to Australia in 1966 from Switzerland and my parents spoke French. I had some delayed speech difficulties due to an early and serious illness of epileptic encephalitis requiring hospitalisation. As I grew old enough to go to preschool, I would return home not speaking English, but French.

Yet I would arrive home and begin singing in English. I used music as the pathway to learning a new language. At primary school I sang in choirs and by the end of primary school I was learning Classical guitar, bewitched by its crystalline tear-drop shaped tone.

At my first lesson, the teacher began explaining the notation to me. *'But I already know!'* I thought, *'You don't need to explain!'*

The guitar was a part of me. I have learnt clarinet, played the piano, and as rewarding and enjoyable as these are, I feel as though I'm playing an instrument, whereas there is a symbiosis with the guitar which makes it an extension of *me*.

Today, in Canberra, Jim and I are performing a half-hour set at a small cafe in Canberra's CBD (Civic) as part of a bushfire fund-raiser.

I have organised our set list, and decide to read three of my poems as well as perform three songs.

There is a small but attentive crowd. After our performance people approach to say how moved they are by my songs and our performance.

I meet a young firefighter who has been fighting fires since August and is utterly exhausted. He keeps referring to this fire season as 'unprecedented'.

I meet a practitioner of Qi Gong who asks the crowd, 'Has anyone here been affected personally by the fires?' Slowly, one, two then four, five, six people raise their hands.

He asks us to step forward. He wants to know how we have been affected.

We stand before him, each taking our turn to respond:

'I am a firefighter, I've been fighting fires since August.'

'I have a sister who has been evacuated five times this season; it has been enormously stressful for herself, her family and all of us.'

'I have asthma and can't breathe properly in the thick smoke that we have endured over this summer.'

'We are from Mallacoota. We lost our home and birds in the bushfires.'

The Qi Gong practitioner, Sunny, asks us to step apart. He explains that in trauma the body can become stuck, and that we can actually release blocked trauma through physical energy and expression of sound. He guides us to sway, wave our arms, and move from side to side, and to express sound vocally. He explains that as trauma gets stuck in the body we disconnect from the body and perhaps cannot feel our legs, or body at all.

'I am made of ash...'

It feel strange to move in this way, with this group of fire-affected strangers. Sunny then invites the audience to join in the movement.

The cafe staff begin to join in as well, as do passers-by. I realize: everyone has been affected by the fires this summer. everyone knows someone who has been affected. Whether you have watched it on the news, or breathed in smoke each day and despaired at the thought of never seeing a blue sky again, or lost a home, or know someone who has, or fought fires, or knows someone who has, or lost a friend or relative to the fires, or know someone who has, or been evacuated five times or have friends that have, or simply missed the pleasure of a day or two at the beach with fish and chips and ice-cream, we have all been affected in some way. We are collectively suffering *solastalgia*...

Music is the great healer. In coming together at this little festival, sharing our fears, our emotions, our experiences, and creating performance to share with others, there is a great healing that can be allowed to take place.

Sunny offers us free bodywork and Qi Gong sessions at his place to help us heal. Thank you, we say. You are very kind...

Our friend Dorothy-Jane has organised a concert at an Art Gallery in Canberra.

We have a one hour set at the end of the evening, following two acts. We don't know who will be in the audience, or what sort of music we will play.

'It will be a listening audience,' Dorothy says.

I decide to perform original songs, mixing blues-jazz genres with some Latin and folk. The gallery is beautifully set up, with lovely lighting, woven rugs on the concrete floors, and chairs and couches arranged intimately around the stage. There is a bar, and tables with platters of food. Outside, there is a barbecue dinner being cooked. The first act is a country style outfit singing harmonies featuring Dorothy-Jane. The second act is Dorothy-Jane singing her poignant and personal blues songs accompanied by guitarist Jeff, followed by an interval. Dorothy announces that people can purchase drinks, a barbecue meal, and other food, and that all proceeds raised tonight will go to Jim and Milena in rebuilding their new life. *All proceeds to Jim and Milena.* I am deeply moved and don't know what to say, how to express my gratitude. Again, kindness...

We launch into our performance. I feel grounded and strong. I know I am connecting with this audience, I can feel it. I also know I am healing, slowly. Each time I perform I am connecting to those hidden parts of myself that are still intact, that haven't been destroyed or lost, and I am rebuilding. Each time I sing I peel back a shredded layer of trauma, anxiety, fear and shock. Each layer that is discarded allows me to reconnect to myself. I know that the music allows others this possibility also. The gallery owner, an awesomely talented artist, shares with me some very personal trauma, expressing her joy at having had the opportunity of some healing through our music. She invites us to attend complimentary art workshops. 'It will be great therapy,' she says.

Again, this thought: *people are kind.*

FEAR

*...fear crept into every corner
of my life.*

Anxiety. Always present, gnawing at my stomach. When I talk I stutter, and my mouth feels frozen, as though concrete has been poured over it and I have to exaggerate the movements to form words. I'm also getting bleeding gums as I keep pushing my teeth into my bottom lip.

Jim and I are arguing incessantly, apart from when we're feeding the magpies on Red Hill.

Everyday I feel overwhelmed, as though there's too much to do and not enough time to do it in. Going to the supermarket, visiting someone, and mailing a parcel feels like a day's work.

I can't sleep. I have strange dreams. I wake too many times during the night. My neck is sore and tight.

I think about life before the house burnt down, and after.

Before. After. As though a line was drawn through my life in black marker pen, on New Year's Eve 2019...

On our way to Brisbane, we stopped for a day at the river in Ballina. Life was beautiful. We drank tea, listened to children play in the park, fed the seagulls, enjoyed a waterfront lunch, relishing the balmy breeze...

On our way back from Brisbane to Canberra, we stopped in the same place at the river in Ballina. We felt the same balmy breeze, heard the children playing, drank tea and fed the seagulls. But this was *after*. I had trouble swallowing my lunch. My gums hurt from pushing my teeth into them. The sea-gulls' screeches irritated me. The children ran too fast. I felt agitated. I was tired...

I have experienced this *before and after* sensation in my life at other times. It comes with sudden shock. Many years ago I experienced a home invasion. As I slept, two armed men in dark balaclavas entered the home, turned on the bedroom light, and stood over my bed. I awoke abruptly, sensing something or someone was in the room. The masked men loomed terrifyingly above me. One had a knife and the other a long steel bar. My worst nightmare was being realised. Trapped, alone, the men were going to rape me, hurt me, then kill me.

My instincts begged me to run, scream, fight. But then I heard my inner voice directing me. *Stay calm. Move slowly. Speak softly.* I felt myself rise above the scene, as though surveying it from above.

I wanted to call the person whose house it was and let them know my predicament. These were pre mobile phone times. As I picked up the receiver to dial, the man holding the knife stepped forward and swiftly sliced the telephone line, leaving me holding the dangling receiver. It was at that point that I realised I was truly alone and that this was a life and death situation.

I was pushed and prodded with the metal bar. The knife was held to my throat. The men wanted money and valuables and were desperately pushing me to give them something.

The home I was in wasn't mine and in actual fact I had simply found myself in the wrong place at the wrong time.

At last, I found a tall canister of money on top of the fridge and that seemed to satisfy them.

They pushed the metal bar into my back, directing me back to the bedroom. They ordered me to get back on the bed. *This is the part where they rape me and kill me*, I thought.

The cold knife was pushed against my throat.

'Breathe a word of this to anyone and we will come back and get you.' With those parting words, they fled. I lay in bed, in shock, completely frozen, listening to the sounds of their footsteps crunching down the gravel driveway until they faded out.

I don't know if the experience had lasted five minutes or fifty, but it felt like hours.

Trembling, I crept to the kitchen, opened the fridge and drank a litre of cold apple juice.

My body went into fight or flight mode and I just wanted to escape. I moved stealthily to the back door, imagining that the men may still be outside somewhere waiting for me to flee.

I was absolutely terrified. I crept like a cat, slinking quietly along the fence line until I reached the back of the garden. Here my instincts took over and I jumped up and over the back fence and began running, tearing my skin on barbed wire on the way.

My heart beating, I entered a friend's house and told him what had just happened.

I insisted on not going back to the house where the break-in had occurred so he drove me to a motel.

For weeks and months I was petrified. I couldn't sleep. I didn't trust any males, I was unable to get in a taxi with a male driver, and still can't to this day. I became hyper-vigilant. I would stand at the window and break out in a sweat if a car stopped on the road with a man or men in it, anywhere near my home. I would hurriedly cross the road if I was walking along the path and two men were approaching. I began carrying a sharp rock in my pocket. I had nightmares, I found it hard to go for a walk alone, even in the middle of the day. I stayed indoors a lot...

My life changed in an instant from *before*. *Before* I had felt safe. Dangerous situations were what happened to other people. They were just stories in a newspaper. *After,* I knew that frightening, dangerous things could happen to anyone, even me, at any time.

And so, when I felt this strong sense of *before* and *after* when we lost our home, it was a familiar feeling. Life was not a constant. Nothing was guaranteed. Things could, and did change at any moment.

After the home invasion, fear crept into every corner of my life. My quality of life was compromised; I could not function as I had before. Eventually, tired of feeling this way, I decided to seek professional help. I saw a trauma counsellor regularly through Victims of Crime Assistance League (VOCAL). The counsellor was gentle, patient and compassionate. She was genuinely interested in helping me reach a positive outcome from my ordeal. Most importantly, she listened, connected and cared. This helped me to gradually and gently unravel the trauma, and to begin to understand that it was possible to move through life again without feeling fearful.

I am booked in for my first session with a psychologist after the bushfires, which has been provided by Cohealth Bushfire Recovery Victoria. My caseworker has organized this and I think it's a positive step towards recovery.

I am apprehensive as I sit in the waiting room to meet her.

Finally I am called. She shakes my hand. Asks me to take a seat. She is not looking at me, but at a piece of paper.

'I need to ask you some questions first,' she says in an official tone.

Continuing to look down and not at me.

'Have you self-harmed or had thoughts of self-harming?'

I look at her blankly. But her eyes don't meet mine.

'Excuse me,' I say, 'I have come here to talk to you about what has happened to me. Do you want to know?'

She looks up at me, for the first time. I begin talking, describing everything that has been going on in my life for the last few months. She looks down and begins writing notes.

When I have finished speaking, she goes back to her form. She looks down again.

'Have you had any thoughts of suicide?'

'Are you having nightmares?'

At the end she explains that whatever I have said today will remain in confidence but if there are concerns they may be shared.

She shakes my hand and asks to see me again in a week.

'That won't be happening,' I think.

The experience feels impersonal, dehumanising. I feel like a number, my stutter exacerbated by her questions. I feel as though I am a subject in a psychology textbook.

I call the office a few days later and cancel further appointments.

My caseworker organises a few relaxation massages for me. I tell him I am craving massage like a thirsty person in the desert craves water.

Takoko, the massage therapist, is a softly spoken Japanese woman with floating movements and a warm smile.

For one and a half hours, in silence, I receive the softest, slowest massage I have ever had in my life. I am normally excessively ticklish and am surprised that I am not jumping off the massage table at the lightness of touch that I am experiencing.

One slow-motion moment followed by another, allowing me to reconnect quietly, deeply, with my core.

At the end of the massage I am calm and sleepy. I sip warm chamomile tea.

After a week or so I realise: *I haven't stuttered this week...*

CANBERRA

...45, what an odd-sounding number.

We are well into a hot February and our time at the motel has come to a close.

I'm grateful to have had a bed and a roof over our heads, but it has been challenging on many levels. Only a microwave to cook meals in, and a small bathroom sink to wash up in, the stress of being in close proximity with my partner every waking moment, strangers knocking loudly on the door at 9am, shouting 'ROOM SERVICE!' too many stairs to climb, exhausted at the end of a long hot day...

On the 7th of February, 2020, a new chapter commences.

We are moving into the house in Holt. No. 45 in a lovely green crescent. *Forty-five. What an odd number*, I think...

Normally, when one moves house, there is a truck, or at least a car full of boxes, and furniture, suitcases and pot-plants. One makes trips back and forth, moving belongings from the old house to the new.

When one loses one's home and everything in it, there is nothing to move. We have six lorikeets, three budgerigars, a few guitars, a *tanaka*, a red teapot, and a backpack or two of clothes.

Friday evening, 7th February, is the first in our big empty house. There is nowhere to sit. We have no couch. No table, no chairs. My son has lent us a thin foam mattress to sleep on. We have purchased two new pillows. Then I realise we have no doona. What will we cover ourselves with?

We have no kettle to make a cup of tea, and no cups to drink it in. We have no teabags.

We have no music, no radio, no television. It is silent.

A friend Jenny, from long ago, with whom I studied guitar, calls me.

'I have some stuff to bring around. Are you there?'

I'm amazed. We had lost touch and I am surprised that she has called me. Her timing is perfect.

An hour later, her car and trailer pulls up in our driveway.

She offloads a round table and four chairs and it fits perfectly in the small dining room.

We have somewhere to sit!

Jenny brings in a small box with sample sized beauty products: miniature bottles of perfume, shampoo, conditioner, face cream. I feel cared for. She gives me a set of Destiny cards in a box.

The idea is that you shuffle them, lay them out in a semi-circle and allow yourself to be drawn to pick one, after asking a question. The card reveals a message to you in answer...

The Destiny cards become my constant companion over the coming few weeks of uncertainty.

The ritual of shuffling and picking a card comforts me, allowing me a moment of stillness and reflection.

My friend Jenny sits on the empty bedroom floor with me and we chat.

Finally, she leaves. A moment later, I hear a knock at the door.

'It's just me again, I forgot I had this for you,' and she hands me a queen-sized doona, cover and two pillowcases.

'*You are the doona fairy,*' I say... I can't believe it. We now have a place to sit, and something to cover ourselves with on the foam mattress.

8th of February. The first morning in our new place. My son arrives with two couches he has found for free online, a rug and a coffee table.

The house feels such a big empty space. Yet I am reluctant to fill it with too many things. Things fill me with anxiety. Too many things mean things to move when it's time again to leave, as I am well aware we will eventually have to do...

I remember my plant in the bathroom in Mallacoota which was just a seedling when I acquired it. It grew so beautiful, glossy and healthy. I feel a pang of grief in my chest and begin to cry...

I want to buy some pot plants. I want life in the house. I go to Bunnings and select four.

It is the end of March. We have been in this house now for almost eight weeks. I don't know where time has gone. Time has evaporated...

Days Roll By

> The days roll by
> My how they fly
> I don't know where my home is
> or how to get there
> But when I get there
> I hope that you come too,
> I hope that someday this dream will come true...
> The nights tick on
> and on and on
> I don't know where my heart is
> or how to find it
> But when I find it
> I hope you will too,
> I hope someday this dream will come true...
> Searching for my anchor
> caught adrift
> But slowly drifting to shore...
> And when I get there
> I hope you'll come too,
> I know that someday this dream will come true...

People have arrived. Donating boxes of things.

A sheet set. Cutlery. A dinner set. Bowls. Jugs. I have been to the Op Shop and returned with four cushions for the couch, and a sky-blue glass bird to place on the windowsill. My mother has sent me a saucepan set for my birthday. My son has given me a charcoal coloured toaster, kettle and a blender for my birthday. I've op-shopped for wine glasses and drinking glasses.

There are doonas and blankets in the cupboard. A lovely and comfortable Ikea armchair in the loungeroom which I've picked up for thirty dollars.

A queen mattress and base ensemble is delivered to us courtesy of a program called 'Mattress for a Mate' for those who lost homes in the fires. We buy ourselves a new bed but for ten weeks we have this one to sleep on until the new one arrives.

I am still living on two minute noodles and ice-cream. I have no inclination to cook.

One day, a friend, Kasia, brings me a jar of three bean soup mix. This simple gesture inspires me to cook a vegetable soup. And so I do. My first home-cooked soup since I left Mallacoota in December, never imagining that it was for the last time...

A house is not a home until you have cooked and shared a meal in it...

HOMESICKNESS

*'There's an ache in my bones,
I want to go home'...*

Homesickness has been whispering at my soul over these past few weeks. I want to sit on our red couch, or maybe our faded blue couch on our front verandah. I want to hear the waves. I want to spend moments immersing myself in the golden green afternoon glow of our backyard. I want to hear Aristotle snorting. I want to go next door and have a cup of tea with my dear neighbours, Bill and Robyn. I want to hop on my bicycle and ride to town, and say hello to this person or that, maybe stop by at Lucy's for her famous dumplings, or the Art Gallery for some visual nourishment...

9 February 2020. It is raining steadily and today is the day that we have chosen to go to Mallacoota. It has been exactly forty days since we lost our home. I can't fathom what it will be like to cast my eyes on the ash, to see for real the horrific photo that I have been trying to process for weeks...

I am scared. I keep imagining that I will arrive and collapse in a crying heap, or begin screaming to the heavens. Or have an anxiety attack so intense that I will find it hard to breathe.

We leave Canberra in the hire car, heading South along the Monaro Highway towards Cooma. Near Bredbo there is charred grass. I see a building half destroyed by fire. As we continue, the scene repeats itself. Over the Brown Mountain it is raining. At Bemboka, there are more blackened paddocks and the remnants of some fire damaged buildings.

Past Eden, we enter a grim apocalyptic landscape. The ground is blackened, as far as the eye can see, to the left and right of us. Spindly black trees stand, spiky and barren, remnants of pre-fire days. There are no birds. It is raining heavily.

At Genoa, we turn left to travel the twenty-three kilometre winding road into Mallacoota. The blackness and smell of death never eases. I stop on the side of the road to exit the car, trying to feel what this dead forest wants to share with me. It is excruciatingly quiet. There is no wildlife. Not an ant, butterfly, or bird to be seen. My heart is heavy. I see a bright green shoot, emerging from the ash and take a photograph of it. *Life in the absence of life.*

Back in the car. I begin to coach myself in an attempt to prepare for the moment we arrive in Mallacoota. *There was a fire.* I think. *Fire is hot. Fire burns things. Many things will have been burnt. Fire doesn't intend to cause harm. It is a scientific fact that flames, fuelled by oxygen, burn things... some of those things were my things. This is a fact. The fire did not carry intent to harm. It simply was.*

I continue talking to myself in this way until we arrive at the sign at the edge of town which says 'Mallacoota! You'll love it!' Such a cheerful and friendly sign in the face of what we are about to encounter.

As we drive into town, things look largely the same as they always have. The inlet is there, as it always has been, a vast silvery expanse of watery splendour framed by the beautiful blue Howe Ranges. It is not really until we reach our street, Betka Road, that we see the extent of the damage. We know that our area was the hardest hit. The fire had raged towards our home across tinder-dry bushland, from the direction of the airport to the South, and our home and those surrounding ours were the first to be devoured by the ravenous monster.

It is raining heavily again. I exit the car and my nostrils are filled with the smell of wet, acrid ash.

I detach completely from the situation emotionally by beginning to take photographs. I can't make sense of what I'm seeing. I'm stumbling around in ash and rubble and bits of roof metal. I don't recognize anything. Nothing makes sense. Our neighbours' homes around us are all destroyed, our fence lines are gone.

At home in Mallacoota I had collected frogs. There were around one hundred and thirty of them, dotted around the home and garden. I stumble upon a green ceramic frog, sitting in the ash as though nothing whatsoever had occurred. Nearby I spot a second, larger clay frog. Apart from these, there is nothing. *Nothing.*

I feel numb. I want to leave. I've had enough, seen enough. I leave Jim who is looking through the rubble and trying to find a way to extricate our Audi TT, miraculously sitting, unblemished, in our neighbour's shed. He needs to find a way to drive it out of the shed over the twisted metal of our neighbour's roof.

I drive around town, with a growing sense of panic. I decide to visit Don Ashby, our friend who had called me on New Year's Eve: *'I've been for a drive, I'm still alive. My home is gone. And so is yours.'*

Visiting Don was always such a great pleasure. His home was an eclectic, artistic clutter of welcome. The large old table was always laid with a vase of flowers, fruit, cheese, olives and homemade bread.

Don always made tea in a pot, never with a teabag. Don had many books, and interesting artwork, much of it his own, on display. The garden was rambling and green, bursting with flowers and herbs, and made me feel as though I was in Provence in the French countryside.

Don's place held some very warm memories for me. We had performed many house concerts there, to appreciative audiences in an intimate setting, the mismatched old wooden chairs adding rustic character. I had also celebrated my fiftieth birthday there, when my father Guido came from Brisbane to visit me, and we had all laughed around the big old table.

This afternoon, as I go in search of Don, I know I cannot go to his beautiful home to find him. His home is gone. Don, always having been the musical and artistic lifeblood of the town, spent a great deal of his time at 'The Muddy'. The Mudbrick Pavillion, affectionately known as 'The Muddy' was Don's second home, and the lighting, sound, and organisation of countless shows over the years have been mostly thanks to Don.

I park outside and walk towards The Muddy, thinking that it's possible that he might be there.

I walk into The Muddy, and there he is, a flurry of bustling energy, as always, packing up after a Cabaret show that I have apparently just missed. 'Don!' I call out.

He looks my way, and we fall into each other's arms. The hug is long and strong, one of solidarity, from another who understands what it means to lose one's home. There isn't much to say. We know.

I then decide to go for a drive. Everything is blackened, it is still raining. There is no wildlife. The streets are empty of people. I call my friend who looked after our birds at home in Mallacoota so beautifully, arrange to meet at 6pm.

I arrive at Lucy's, Mallacoota's famous dumpling house. It is almost empty. Someone approaches me, explaining that we are entitled to a free cup of coffee because we lost our home. The coffee comes. I don't feel like it but I suppose I will have to drink it. Someone brings a form and asks us to sign it to say we've received our coffee. The whole process feels contrived. I don't enjoy the coffee. 'Here, your house burnt down, have a free coffee...'

I think back to a young man in Brisbane, an apprentice mechanic, who fitted new tyres on our Oka courtesy of the Oka Owners Group, which contacted us to ask if we needed any help after our home burnt down. They offered to fit new tyres on our vehicle, which we gratefully accepted. When we arrived at the workshop to pick up the Oka, the young apprentice approached me shyly at the window, and said, 'I heard what happened to you, I would like to give you this, buy yourselves a coffee', and handed me a crumpled five dollar note, probably just enough for his icy cold knock-off beer... He was so genuine, humble, and the gesture made my heart swell with gratitude at his thoughtfulness...

I have an urgent desire to get out of this town. We had planned to stay a night, maybe two, but I have seen my friend, she has kindly given us some blankets and a care pack of non-perishable food, and we've had dinner. Now I want out.

The drive back to Canberra is around four hours. It is getting dark. We will be home by midnight if we leave now. I am in the hire car, Jim is following behind me in the Audi. I haven't driven for almost six years until last week, and it's not my car. I have just surreally experienced seeing nothing where my home once stood... I begin to drive. It starts pouring heavily with rain. I sing, trying to stay focused. I am agitated and nervous. I sing:

> *I've got peace like a river*
> *I've got peace like a river in my soul.*

Still nervous...

> *I've got love like an ocean*
> *I've got love like an ocean in my soul.*

Still anxious...

> *I've got joy like a fountain*
> *I've got joy like a fountain in my soul.*

Still agitated. A vision of the rubble enters my mind suddenly, a flash of ash. My tears begin streaming like the pouring rain. I start to sing a song that I make up on the spot about the birds. I am singing goodbye to our beautiful birds who did not deserve to die this awful, horrific death. I sing for each one, sobbing through my song, tears flowing down my cheeks as rain flows across my windscreen. I am not in control. I am anxious, agitated. I feel I will crash the car if I continue driving. Four hours of driving feels an insurmountable challenge. I pull over, signalling for Jim to pull over too.

'I can't keep going,' I say.

'What?' he says, 'We could have stayed in Mallacoota and saved money!'

'I don't care about the money. I am going to write myself off and the car too if we keep going. I'll just book into this Motel at Cann River and we can head off in the morning.'

After a couple of hours drinking tea, eating chocolate and lazing about we drift off to sleep and wake refreshed for the trip back to Canberra.

From Cann River we head out past Noorinbee towards Bombala. Again, we are confronted by mile after mile of dead, bleak, blackened bush. There is nothing! Devastation as far as the eye can see. The sheer magnitude of this disaster overwhelms me.

There are no birds.

Approaching Canberra, I am so grateful in the reassuring knowledge that we have a house to return to. If we had been returning to the motel room, or a friend's couch perhaps, coping with everything we've just had to absorb might have felt insurmountable. At least we have a house. I can't call it a home yet, as it is temporary and everything is new. But it is shelter.

Shelter from the storm...

GIFTS

... make some beautiful sounds

Random packages without a return address keep appearing at our front door. I have never opened so many packages. Packages of tea, and teacups, packages of music books, tea-towels and towels: our new life in boxes.

When a box arrives at the doorstep it is accompanied by an immediate stress response. The stress of not knowing what is in the box, the stress of opening the box and disposing of the cardboard. The stress of having to deal with what is in the box and find a spot for it in the home. The stress of the idea of dealing with what is in the box when, ultimately, we have to leave this house for a new one, yet again.

I have never had so many bowls. People keep giving us bowls. I like bowls. Bowl food is comfort food. Bowls hold steaming hot homemade soups on a chilly Autumn evening, creamy warm porridge on a cold Winter's morning, fresh fruit salad on a hot Summer's night.

My friend Costanza has delivered a beautiful and enormous hand-made pottery bowl, in white and blue. I place it, empty, on the sideboard. It remains empty until I receive a package at the front door of percussion instruments. I arrange the instruments in the bowl, which has now become a musical bowl.

Our friend Sean comes for a visit, and brings us a large floral ceramic bowl in blues, greens, and whites. I adore it. I fill it with apples, bananas, oranges and tomatoes. It is a beautiful bright centrepiece in the kitchen.

For my birthday, my sister gives me four dark blue and sky blue oriental bowls, for eating spaghetti, rice or cereal.

I have large white ceramic mixing bowls, ready to hold a pancake batter for my granddaughter or a chocolate cake for guests, or to soak lentils in for a curried soup, or cracked wheat for a refreshing, colourful tabouli salad.

I have a bright red glazed bowl, perfect to hold a couple of scoops of glistening green olives.

I have bowls which are part of a dinner set which my friend gifted me. He asked me to choose a dinner set. I looked endlessly at classic white dinner sets, angular sets, floral sets, and bright, cheerful ones, before settling on a set named *'ecology'* of a grey green mist colour. The bowls look so beautiful holding a silky, golden pumpkin soup with a swirl of cream on top.

Bowls are receptacles for nourishment and comfort. Bowls are offerings of love... thank you for my bowls.

There is an organisation that I learn about called Resound. Resound links musical instruments to musicians who have lost theirs in the fires. Early on, whilst still in Brisbane, I make a list of those we have lost, of which there are many, and submit it to Resound.

The list contains not only instruments, but my entire library of classical guitar music which I've gathered since the age of fourteen or so, a lifetime of music...

At our house in Holt, a box arrives at the door one morning. It is heavy. I have no idea what's in it. I open it with a hint of anxiety and see it contains reams of guitar music.

So much music begging to be played! Silent notes waiting to be transformed into music by human flesh.

I spend a day organising and then reorganising the music into alphabetical order.

I am so grateful...

There is a knock at the door. A lady turns up with instruments. I don't know who she is or where she is from. She hands me an old Yamaha classical guitar. And a clarinet in a case. A small guitarlele (a cross between a guitar and a ukelele). A mandolin. I am overwhelmed. I cannot cope with the sudden influx of instruments. I feel swamped. Too many boxes! Too many things! I am sweating, my heart is racing.

The joy is in the *choosing*. Of entering a music store, trying this guitar then that, of finding a guitar that resonates with the heart, and of being unable to put that particular guitar down, drawn to its tone and feel under my fingers.

The excitement of taking it to the counter, knowing it will be accompanying me home.

Or the delight of browsing an op shop, stumbling upon a mandolin, inlaid with mother of pearl hummingbirds, and bartering the price down a few dollars... Of course, I am grateful that someone has come to our door bearing instruments, yet I'm confused as I don't recall why or how she came to be here, and there are too many instruments arriving too fast, like too much food at an all you can eat buffet dinner when you're not really hungry. Stressed, always stressed since we lost our home.

I open the clarinet. It has a handwritten note in it:

> 'To the musical person who will make this clarinet play beautiful sounds again. I am so sorry that you have lost everything due to the horrific fires. I am saddened for your loss of your treasured valuable things but rest assured you have loving caring family friends and new friends who will help you rebuild your life in weird and wonderful ways. Hold those dearest to you a little closer and step back occasionally to appreciate the small things in life. We all have control of our lives and now it's your turn to rebuild change a few things and follow your dreams. A little about this clarinet! It was given to me about 40 years ago by my parents, I am the youngest of six children and the only one who learnt to play an instrument. Why? I am a chronic asthmatic and it was said it would help my breathing. I must admit that sport was more interesting to me so only played during my primary school days. I treasured it for all these years simply because my parents sacrificed a lot for me to learn to play, not just time and money but their ears!! Oh my! I can still hear the squeak when first learning to play. I encouraged my own children to play but they were not interested. So my dear recipient of this lovely clarinet, make some beautiful sounds.
>
> Kindest regards Alison'

Alison. Who are you? Where are you? How do I thank you? You are kind.

I recall, suddenly, that after the fires I had applied to Resound and listed some of our lost instruments. That is how the lady bearing instruments appeared at our front door. It is kind of her. I feel bad for feeling stressed. I think of those who have lost everything and perhaps have no friends, or no computer to find out about organisations such as Resound. Those who are lonely. Or in bad health. Or who still haven't found a place to reside.

I think of the refugees, who have come from war-torn countries, seeking safety. Those who have lost everything, family members included perhaps, displaced, traumatised. Who are then placed in indefinite detention and treated inhumanely. No wonder there is self-harm. No wonder they want to die. No wonder they take their own lives or go slowly and surely insane.

I am grateful. Grateful for this house, for my family, my partner, for the guitar, the mandolin and the clarinet.

Grateful.

QUEEN CORONA

Strange times indeed

I am no stranger to moving home. From the time I was born until I left school I had lived in ten houses, two of those in a foreign country, and three of those in different cities.

From the time I left home, until now, I can count fifteen. Twenty-five moves altogether. That averages out to a change of home every 2.2 years.

I'm fortunate to have found a place we can call our own for a while, but in the back of my mind is the constant knowledge that we have a one-year lease here in Canberra, by which time we will need to have either rebuilt a place, or bought a house somewhere, in the hope that the land in Mallacoota will sell by then. Life has thrown a new obstacle at us though, and it has meant that our best laid plans have been put on hold, along with the rest of the world's...

Her name is coronavirus and she causes a disease called Covid-19.

On December 31 2019, the same night our home was taken by fire in Mallacoota, China reported several cases of a rather aggressive form of pneumonia in the port city of Wuhan, in the province of Hubei in Central China, to the World Health Organisation (WHO). It was reported that several of those cases of infection could be traced back to workers from the Huanan Seafood Market, which was subsequently shut down on January 1 2020.

By the January 7 it was announced officially by WHO that a new virus had been identified. It belonged to a group of viruses known as Corona, spread by being in proximity to an infected person and inhaling droplets spread by coughing, sneezing or touching an infected surface.

By January 11 China had reported its first mortality from the virus, and on January 13 WHO announced that a case in Thailand had occurred when a woman arrived in Thailand from Wuhan.

Cases began to be reported in France, Australia, South Korea, Vietnam, Singapore, Malaysia and Taiwan, with China reporting their third fatality by January 20.

Measures were swiftly taken by Asia to help block the spread of the virus, including mandatory screenings at airports of arrivals from China. By January 22, China's death toll had jumped to seventeen, with more than five hundred and fifty infections. Wuhan was placed into quarantine, and large and popular Lunar New Year events were cancelled. News stories began emerging of residents' homes being welded shut by police to prevent their leaving. Hong Kong quickly followed suit, declaring a virus emergency and closing down Lunar New Year's Events.

On January 30, WHO declared a global emergency due to coronavirus. By January 31, exactly one month after we lost our home, the number of infected in China rose to 9809 and Europe began reporting its first cases of the virus. On February 1, Australia confirmed its first case.

By February 9, the day we made the necessary but intensely difficult journey back to Mallacoota, China's death toll had surpassed that of the 2002-2003 SARS epidemic.

On Feb 11, WHO named the new coronavirus Covid-19. Around this time the death toll in China had jumped to 1,300 with almost 60,000 infected.

On February 21, the region of Lombardy in Italy reported the first local transmission of coronavirus leading to Covid-19, with six infected.

By the end of February, global cases numbered 80,000 and fatalities neared 2,800 world wide.

By 8 March the Italian government imposed a strict quarantine as numbers of infections became the highest worldwide, closely followed by Iran. On March 10, in a single day, one hundred and sixty-eight deaths were recorded in Italy alone. My cousin Silvia, in lockdown in Italy, began writing to me, describing what was going on in very real and personal terms. She explained that the Italian people were not allowed out, apart from for essentials (medicine and food). She told me that her close friend had recently died in a car crash and she could not even go and mourn him at his funeral, and that her brother Massimo had lost his job as a pilot with Alitalia. Although only a few kilometres away, she could not go and visit him.

It was on March 11, with an ever-growing list of countries reporting a rapid spread of coronavirus infections, that WHO declared the outbreak a pandemic.

On March 19, Italy overtook China with the most deaths worldwide. Hospitals were reported to be overflowing with people being treated in corridors, and doctors were having to make the terrible decision about who would live and who would die as their medical system was at breaking point.

The United States, the UK, and Spain began to report ever increasing cases, with Spain reporting 39,673 cases and 2,182 fatalities.

Here, in Australia, our world began to change as the government began implementing strategies to prevent a surge of cases, and to 'flatten the curve' by advising that people remain home wherever possible unless going out for exercise, essential shopping, or medical appointments. Clubs, pubs, places of worship, gyms, pools, casinos, nightclubs, cinemas and entertainment venues were shut, as were beauty parlours, massage and tattoo parlours, outdoor and indoor markets, galleries, libraries, indoor sports venues, public playgrounds and skate-parks. Restaurants and cafés could remain open but strictly for takeaway only. Hand sanitiser became the most prized item in society, and induced by a flurry of panic buying, supermarket shelves became completely empty of hand sanitiser, soap, toilet paper and tissues.

Around the third week of March, the shelves began emptying of canned beans, canned tomatoes, tomato paste, pasta, rice, flour and milk. Shortly after this, supplies of mince meat and parmesan cheese began to dwindle. It was, it appeared, on all Australians' minds to cook what appeared to have become the national dish during the pandemic: spaghetti bolognese.

This was clearly demonstrated when I made a trip to the supermarket to buy tomato paste and parmesan cheese. Jars of tomato paste had sold out, and there were only small sachets in a box available. I went to purchase two boxes which I thought would be almost the equivalent to one jar, plus a container of parmesan, as I wanted to cook minestrone for my son and his wife who had given birth to my granddaughter Violet on the fourteenth of March against the backdrop of this pandemic.

'You'll have to put one of those items back,' the cashier announced.

'Sorry?' I said.

He repeated the phrase again.

'But why?' I asked.

'They're in the same category. You're only allowed two items in the same category.'

'But one is cheese, the other is tomato, how can that be the same category?' I argued.

'The computer has put it all together in the spaghetti bolognese category,' he announced.

'But I'm not making spaghetti bolognese!' I explained. 'I'm making minestrone!'

'Sorry madam. The computer has decided.'

I put the parmesan back, bought my tomato paste, and walked out, defeated by a computer.

A few days later, I went to buy paper towel ready to have next to soap at our house-warming party. There were two packs, sitting side by side, on a completely bare shelf. I went to reach for one packet. An elderly couple suddenly appeared out of nowhere next to me, and glared at me violently. Such was the intensity of their glare that I stepped back. They grabbed the two packets of paper towel and marched out, on a mission. People can be kind: but in times of crisis, where people experience fear and stress, they can react in thoughtless and selfish ways, where nothing matters but their own needs.

Alarmingly, I was in the same supermarket a few days later, and a young man pulled a knife out on one of the cashiers. He was shouting and waving it about. I stood, frozen on the spot, until the police were called and he was led away by store security, still ranting.

I noted that at the supermarket, people looked grim-faced and stressed. I would smile at people, but for the first time in my life, no one seemed to smile back...

Strange times indeed...

On March 29, the government announced a further wave of restrictions. People were ordered not to gather publicly in groups of more than two. People over the age of seventy were strongly advised to stay home, along with those over sixty suffering from chronic illness, and indigenous Australians over the age of 50. Weddings were restricted to five people in total, and funerals to ten. Auctions and open house inspections were banned. Some of Australia's beaches were officially closed, for example all of Mornington Peninsula's beaches, as well as some of Sydney's, which were also patrolled by police helicopters.

A ban on overseas travel was put in place and any overseas arrivals were immediately taken by police escort to compulsory fourteen-day quarantine at city hotels. Western Australia, South Australia, and the Northern Territory and Queensland had all closed their borders.

The impact on the entertainment industry, and the Hospitality and Tourism sectors, will be enormous: economically the effects on Australia (and indeed the world) may prove catastrophic, considering the economic fallout of the 'Lost Summer' of drought and bushfires which already had significantly impacted tourism and small business in Australia. Most communities along the eastern seaboard had been ravaged by a fiery and relentlessly savage Summer. Autumn and Easter were a time when people were looking forward to recovery, to opening their fire-ravaged towns back to tourists, to celebrating the close of a traumatic summer. Small and large music festivals which generated large numbers of visitors to coastal communities were systematically cancelled. *The Lost Summer* had now been closely followed by The Lost Autumn, and Winter was gearing up to be the peak of infection time, where the most cases of Covid-19 were likely to hit our population.

Bushfire-affected people seemed to have been forgotten. Queen Corona reigned supreme and all were bowing, trembling, to her power. Society seemed to have gone from one of kindness towards bushfire victims: 'What can we do to help you?' to one of 'Out of my way, I need this, and you don't matter'. In fact, it seemed that people had all but forgotten, if they weren't directly affected, just how traumatic the Summer had been for those impacted...

It is March 30. We have been in self-isolation here, in our new house, for a fortnight now. We are very fortunate to have a house to be isolated in. Some don't. I wonder about homeless people, how they can self-isolate, how they can keep safe, how they can eat, and stay warm. We have a front verandah, and a back one also. We have a garden. We have a loungeroom, a dining room. We have food in our fridge, and a warm bed to sleep in. I have a guitar to practise on, donated after the fires, and a computer to write on, also donated, which has enabled me to fill my quiet time by writing these pages... I wonder about those traumatised by the fires, by the loss of their homes, still stressed, anxious and unsettled emotionally, not able to focus on recovery now because of the added stress of this pandemic. Life can and does change swiftly; it only takes an instant.

On this day exactly a year ago, I was performing a CD and book launch in collaboration with a group of fine musicians after I had set a book of published poems by John Passant to song. To an audience of almost a hundred, we played our hearts out. The poet was present and read some of his poems. At the end there was much hugging and celebrating. Never in my wildest imagination could I have guessed that exactly a year later, our Mallacoota home would be a pile of ash, our birds would be deceased, hugging would be disallowed, music would not be played publicly, and that we would be living in a home in Canberra, in lockdown.

I also couldn't have imagined that John Passant's life would cease, sadly, a year later, on 6 April 2020. That despite the thousands of tributes flowing in for this incredibly loved man, tragically, because of Covid-19 regulations, only seven people would attend his funeral. Jim and I were honoured to be able to attend and to sing a song for our beloved friend John at the conclusion of the service.

Each day I dread the ticking of time and the eventual inevitable move that must once again be made, to yet again a new place. Coupled with the uncertainty of the dark times we are experiencing and of what the aftermath will be, we are also faced with the uncertainty of where we will go, what we will do. I try to enjoy this lovely new house, which is our shelter from the storm, but the knowledge that this will inevitably cease depresses and preoccupies me. Yesterday I cried and cried at the thought of moving yet again. I am not sure I can bear it. I try and focus on the present. I keep telling myself:

Each moment must be savoured.

Over the course of time it becomes apparent that the reign of Queen Corona is far from over: there appears to be a second, or even a third wave; suffice to say that the number of infections and deaths continue to mount daily, in their hundreds of thousands, creating fear and uncertainty globally.

At the time this book went to print at end July 2020, 18 million cases of the virus had been recorded globally. In Australia, there were 16,000 cases recorded. Borders had closed between New South Wales and Victoria, and South Australia and Victoria. The city of Melbourne was in complete lockdown, with the wearing of masks outdoors mandatory for all Victorians. Economically, Australia had fallen into recession by Julys' end, with estimated predictions of one or 2 out of 10 Australians jobless by the close of the year.

Her Majesty Corona has changed the world as we know it, and she will forever be a part of the history of the year 2020, and beyond ...

Trolley Man

...home ... a trolley with a few meagre possessions

It is now already April.

My cousin Silvia, still in quarantine in Rome, writes to me: 'We are locked down for another month at least; I am at home. I can't see the twins who live with their father because they can't leave their home. Police patrol the streets and a month ago they were leaving my place and two officers stopped them and nearly fined them. Nobody can move from home; you can move with a declaration stating that there is an emergency or if you need to buy food. Just kids under eighteen can be visited by their parents in cases of separation. Mine are adults and if they come here, their driver licence can be confiscated, and they can be reported and fined. No one can leave home unless there is a proven emergency. This is a pandemic and the measures are very strict. I am so glad to see you have managed to create a new home, I imagine how hard all these months have been for you. But you are strong and creative. Stronger than fire...

Love, Silvia'

Last night on the news, I watched in horror, scenes from New York, and increasingly, other states in the United States, where makeshift hospitals are being erected in empty buildings and sporting grounds.

I watched footage of street after street lined with tents belonging to a proportion of the half million homeless that make up America's population. For those fortunate to have a tent, it provides some semblance of shelter from the elements. For those that don't, there is increased threat of violence, cold, damp and sickness...

Homelessness as defined by *The McKinney-Vento Homelessness Assistance Act*, a United States Federal Law established in 1987, is 'the condition of people lacking a fixed, regular, and adequate night-time residence'.

Essentially, to define homelessness one must first define home. A home is not only a physical space, walls and a roof. Ideally, it provides a sense of identity, well-being, security and history. It is a place that one can return to with a sense of belonging and connectedness, time and time again.

When home is lost suddenly, for reasons such as poverty, domestic violence, mental health issues and natural disasters, one becomes adrift, anchorless.

Homelessness may induce additional conditions such as mental and physical health issues and substance addiction which exacerbate the situation.

Typically, in Western countries, single males comprise eighty percent of homeless populations.

In Australia there are currently around 100,000 homeless, sleeping in sheltered doorways and back-streets.

Last night as I lay in my warm bed in our temporary four bedroom house, my mind wandered to the world's homeless. With the global directive induced by the Covid-19 pandemic being 'You should be staying home!' for the world's homeless this is not possible.

To stay home and isolate under ones country's directives is a privilege not afforded to all.

Joseph Cindric (1906-1994) The Sydney Trolley Man.

If you were a Sydney-sider who regularly frequented the City around Hyde Park and Martin Place during the 1970s and 1980s, then you may recall the slightly stooped figure of a man wearing a long coat, a construction helmet and pushing a handmade trolley around the CBD.

He was as much a part of Sydney's city scene during these decades as the Town Hall, or the pigeons in Hyde Park where the man often slept or wandered during the day.

This was Joseph Cindric. Whilst he lived, almost nobody knew his name. He was an elusive but constant feature in Sydney city. People passed his familiar face each day without saying hello for years.

Immigration records from the National Archive indicate that the Sydney Trolley Man was born Josef Cindric, in 1906 in former Yugoslavia, arriving in Sydney on October 1948, and classed as a displaced person, or a refugee.

Records indicate that he was a qualified ships' engineer. Due to challenges in adapting to life in Australia including language barriers, which led to an increasing inability to hold down employment, Cindric began wandering the streets from the 1960s.

Synonymous with Joseph Cindric was his trolley. Handmade by Cindric himself, the trolley was an ever-changing work in progress, at its height in the mid-70s, rolling on motorcycle wheels, and shrinking in size in the mid-80s when Cindric's health began declining.

Cindric carried his belongings on his trolley. These were clothes and personal belongings, letters from his sons in Europe, and tools or scavenged and donated parts essential for repairs to keep the trolley rolling along.

Cindric became known for the construction helmet that he began wearing constantly after being mugged one night in Hyde Park whilst he was sleeping. He took to sleeping during the day and wandering during the night to prevent a further night-time attack.

On August 29 2010, Lorne Johnson from Sydney posts on the Museum of Applied Arts and Sciences website in the comments section of an article about Cindric:

> 'I've been spooked/bedazzled by Cindric since being a child on Sydney's streets in the 70s and 80s. My school mates and I dubbed him 'Red Helmet' because he predominantly wore that colour helmet, not the white, when I saw him the most. I think the white helmet turned up closer to his death. I once asked him for directions at Lang Park (Wynyard area) and he gave them to me in a slurred, dismissive manner. I remember he looked like a misplaced cosmonaut or firefighter. He had prominent ears and his tongue was often out slightly when he was asleep. I miss his ambiguous soul on Sydney's streets.'

Joseph Cindric has inspired artists of various mediums to write, film, sculpt or sing about him.

Lorne Johnson has written a piece on the subject of Cindric published by *Mascara Literary Review*:

Trolley Man

For over twenty years you pushed your trolley between
Sydney's glass and chrome
with a red crash helmet protecting your imagination from
having a head on with reality.
Hunched like Atlas during his nursing home years, villagers
who worship rice,
you were this bitumen Bedouin who'd arrived from the far
corners of abstraction,
never the Central Business District's central business, but
always mine.

Your ambiguity unhinged me: your tongue carried the weight
of bedlam's flare, your
ubiquitous presence provided this surrogate backbone
through my edgy Marist
testosterone years. Along with the Monorail's click-clack-
glide-hum, Club 77's pop arc,

the hanging whale geometry in the Australian Museum foyer,
neon-smacked vegetable
boxes in Dixon Street and whispers within St Mary's gothic
skin, you were my Sydney.

Your origins and the contents of your trolley were the stuff of
Holt's conclusion.
The dove-hearted who fed the wandering bed cravers said you
were a shipwright and a
knife sharpener. Homeless men with ashy cigar toes and Orc
profiles said your trolley
contained old letters and photos from a frozen bullet you'd
fled. To open truth, one
would have to make a point of cross-questioning the pointers
of The Southern Cross.

The only certainty is that in 'nineteen ninety-four, you pushed
your fading street-life
into the gardens between The Domain and the cool jade
lapping that defines us. Amidst
weaves of lush multicultural foliage, under a sweaty scarlet sky
cooled by the wing flap
of fruit bats, you sat facing The Bridge's inverted robot-smile,
shut your eyes and waited
for the long golden afternoon to cave in on you and your
bright dancing secrecy.

Lorne Johnson 2008
(quoted with permission)

In 1994, Joseph Cindric, Sydney's iconic trolley man, died alone and homeless. He was buried at Rookwood Cemetery in Sydney. Although known to so many Sydneysiders, in attendance at his funeral were two nurses and artist Richard Goodwin, who, fascinated by Cindric's existence and his relationship with his all important trolley, photographed and filmed Cindric for many years, and subsequently produced exhibitions on the subject.

My heart aches for the man, who led such a public but lonely life.

I wrote a song for Cindric after reading about him in the book by Australian novelist Delia Falconer entitled *Sydney*:

Cindric's Trolley

You shuffle the streets stooped and tired
past beggars and smells and bad hotels
Pushing your way through the lunchtime crowds
stopping to rest on a bench in the park
waiting for daylight to fade into dark

People try not to stop and stare
what is that on your head that you wear?
you were beaten one night in the dark
and a helmet's your only salvation

On a trolley you push all your worldly possessions
scraps, clothes, letters and tools
its silent wheels are your only friend
on its frame you depend
it accompanies you through the darkness of night
and is still by your side with the dawning of light

There's men like you in every city
others look on from afar with pity
Nobody stops to ask you your name
share in some time, see if you're fine
nobody asks why you don't have a home
nobody cares that you ceaselessly roam

Where do you come from?
Where do you go?
Nobody knows nobody knows...

And when your time comes and they wave you farewell
and they put you under the ground
who will be there to honour your life?
no one, no one
your trolley will stop
on the day that you die
never to roll again, never to roll again

Where did you come from?
Where did you go?
Nobody knows nobody knows...

Milena Cifali February 2016
from album 'Poplar Road'

I vividly remember another 'trolley man' I met in my youth.

Unlike Joseph Cindric, the man, whom I only remember as 'Mark', made a choice to become homeless...

I met him in Garema Place in the late seventies, in Canberra. A stage with loudspeaker was set up on Saturday mornings where people could get up and have their say on any topic.

It was at this Saturday morning soapbox that I met Mark. Upon sitting and chatting over the course of a few weeks, I learnt that he was a radio presenter with a Canberra commercial radio station, also worked in advertising and was what one would describe as a 'successful' twenty-something year old.

His father had been in the Army and Mark had felt that growing up in that environment had been stifling and restrictive.

Mark was married and had a young child. At some point in the early eighties, he decided to renounce what he saw as the 'trappings of success' and decided that he would survive on the left-over food of others, discarded on café plates, and on food that he would find in hoppers and garbage bins, and that with a trolley and a few clothes he would live as a wandering nomad, walking around Australia. He threw away his surname, cancelled all his credit cards and bank accounts, and asked his wife to join him. She was not enthusiastic and eventually they separated.

Five years later, travelling to Cape York, I spotted the hunched figure of a man walking slowly alongside the highway as we were coming into Port Douglas. *'That's Mark,'* I thought... I pulled over, rolled down the window and asked, 'Are you Mark?'

'Yes I am,' he replied.

Incredibly, 2,565km and five years from Canberra, Mark was standing in front of me with his trolley and the few clothes he owned. He explained that he was surviving still on the leftovers that people left on their plates, and that he would simply go up to a table and ask, 'Have you finished with that?'

He was also living from fruit that he picked from trees growing in people's gardens, in orchards or growing wild.

Mark the trolley man was a world apart from Joseph Cindric the trolley man. Their life circumstances and what led them to be pushing a trolley around the streets were entirely different. Yet for both of these men, home meant a trolley with a few meagre possessions, and providing the trolley was still by their side when they awoke in the morning, then presumably some semblance of connectedness to the concept of home existed for them both...

The Oka

...we were home

When Jim's mother died in 2011 he decided to purchase something he'd always dreamed of owning with his inheritance. An Oka.

OKA Motor Company was an Australian company that began making four-wheel drive tour buses in Western Australia in 1986, with a production output of approximately five hundred.

OKAs ran mostly on the four-cylinder Perkins phaser engine. In 1999 Malaysian manufacture of OKA commenced, but in 2011 OKA was placed in administration, and an attempt to recapitalise was unsuccessful so operations ceased.

Our Oka was number 325. The Oka was big and high and sturdy.

We could fit all our instruments and PA gear into it, as well as our birds, and travel wherever the road took us, or wherever we decided to share our music.

Everywhere we travelled people would stop and ask, 'What sort of vehicle is that?'

... or 'I've always wanted one of those!'

... or 'You two are living the dream!'

After a year or so, Jim took all the seats out of the bus and built us a bed in the back of the Oka. In that instant, the first night our heads hit the pillow, our Oka became our second home.

There was such beauty in stopping alongside a beach or river, and crawling into the back of the bus into the comfort of our own bed, and lying quietly in the stillness with the curtain drawn back and the windows open to allow the cool sea breeze to caress our faces, the sound of the waves in our ears lulling us to sleep, and the sight of a thousand glittering stars in the big blackness inspiring awe.

At sunrise, I would sit up, forgetting where we were, and be greeted at the sight of the ocean awash in morning colours, or the forest resounding with a hundred bird calls.

I would step outside, into the new day, stretch and breathe deeply.

This same ritual of night and day in our Oka was always a beautiful new happening even when it occurred over and over.

In the Oka we had our clothes, our birds, an old wooden army box with cans of food and spices and tea. I had a basket full of jewellery. We had our toothbrushes, our towels, our shoes, some books, and maps. The Oka was home when we were away from Mallacoota.

In the Oka we travelled along the Great Ocean Road of Victoria, along the wild and windswept coast of South Australia, to Adelaide and up through the centre of South Australia, travelling North towards the Red Centre. We drove in to Woomera, deep in the South Australian desert and performed music at The Eldo Hotel (European Launcher

Development Organisation), which before becoming a Hotel was the headquarters for the former European space research organisation.

We drove on to Alice Springs, and headed out to Uluru to be awed at the power of the enormous red monolith, which seemingly breathes with life:

Kapi Mutijulu

Kapi Mutijulu, sacred stillness,
it's the red rock shouting to the blue sky
Uluru is power!

It's water in a deep green pool
Tumbling to Kapi below,
It's the golden light, an eagle in flight,
The caressing breeze,
Being at ease, timeless.

It's the sun on my face, a sense of this place,
It's the Serpent Dreaming,
The desert meaning,
It's painted rock, red to gold,
red sand in my palm to hold, timeless.

It's a black cockatoo, it's a didgeridoo,
The desert air heavy with peace,
A bush caterpillar on a leaf,
A billion stars in the deep night sky,
I wonder why it makes me cry, timeless...

It's the old ghost gum,
A Universal hum,
The earth is my mother,
The sun is my brother,
The moon she's our sister,
Listen to the spirits whisper.
Timeless...

Listen to the country,
Listen to the stories...
The red dirt gets into your veins washes away all your pains,
washes away all your pains.

Kapi Mutijulu, sacred stillness,
It's the red rock shouting to the blue sky,
Uluru is power!

We drove in The Oka to the emerald green forests and golden beaches of Northern New South Wales and Queensland. We drove in the Oka many times, back and forth, from Mallacoota to Eden, then Bermagui, via the magnificent cathedral-like spotted gum forest that rolls down to the ocean:

> I Belong Here
> Lyrics Milena Cifali
> The tall spotted gums
> sweep down to the sea
> kissing her shores majestically
> harbouring life in all of its forms
> koalas cockatoos parrots and wallabies.
> And if you listen closely
> you can hear the forest sing
> I belong here for all time

> I belong here this life is mine.
> Protected by the Spirit of Gulaga,
> Sacred mother to young and old,
> Custodian of this magic place,
> Why would anyone want to deface her?
> And if you listen closely
> you can hear the forest sing
> I belong here for all time
> I belong here this life is mine.
> I belong, this life is mine.

We drove the high country, to Tumbarumba, in mid-winter, past gurgling creeks in thick eucalyptus forest under brilliant blue skies, the sun on the leaves creating diamonds.

We drove out West in NSW, through small country towns like Booroowa and Cowra, Forbes, Parkes and Canowindra, where old men still politely tip their hats and say 'good day' when you pass them on the footpath. Where old utes pull up with a couple of kelpies or blue heelers in the back, tired from rounding up sheep. Where there are always two pubs, one on each corner, but the farmers each have their favourite local and would never in a million years venture across the road to the other pub to get their beer. Where the take-away reliably makes fish and chips, even though the ocean is miles away.

We drove along Beach Road in Melbourne, admiring the grand Victorian architecture on one side and the shimmering silver expanse of Port Phillip Bay on the other, ever changing, depending on the weather, the light and the time of day...

We drove the crowded and frantic streets of Sydney City, crossing the Harbour Bridge, to the Northern Beaches.

We drove the vast flat moonscape of the Monaro, the endless sky always larger than life, the yellow plains and grey steel skies lit dramatically as though here was a staged production: Big Sky Country.

We drove and drove, and drove some more. Whether in the mountains or on the coast, in the forest or the desert, the countryside, villages, or the city, we could just pull over somewhere quiet in our Oka, crawl into the back, and have a moment's rest, or a night's replenishing sleep.

Although we lost our home and everything in it on 31 December 2019, fortunately we had one Oka, nine birds, one guitar and one bass with us, that survived. As did we.

We were home.

GRIEVING

*Home is in the heart but
you will never find your way back....*

Today I'm grieving. It's April 15 2020 and it has been many weeks since we lost our home.

A photo of my indigo blue bottles on the windowsill in Mallacoota sets me off. I am starting to realise, with time, that our home is not there anymore. It really did incinerate along with everything in it. There really is nothing left. The grief hits hard, like a punch in the chest, abrupt, intense.

Here I was feeling that I was healing, that things were okay. And they are, really. But grief is like that, it comes in waves, like sets rolling in on the beach, first a few small waves and then *crash!* out of the blue a big wave that comes out of nowhere, catching you by surprise, knocking you off your feet, taking your breath away and making you lose your sense of equilibrium...

And then, guilt. I look around at this lovely house, the kindness of people that have donated things, the garden, the magpies, our comfortable bed. How dare I feel grief when I am so fortunate? When I am still alive whilst others didn't make it?

Nevertheless, today, I feel grief...

This lovely house and most of the things in it were given to us.

At home, in Mallacoota, most of what we owned was *chosen*.

It was us who thought *yes, we will buy this home and settle here*. It was us who went couch shopping and of all the thousands of couches in existence chose two red leather ones. It was us that placed our chosen books, gathered over a lifetime, on our white bookshelves, that we chose, and assembled. It was us who planted chosen succulents in our garden, and us that chose to rip out the carpet and replace it with floorboards when we moved in...

Everywhere I look, in each corner of the house in Holt, I see the loving gestures of friends and strangers who were kind enough to pause their daily routines to post us this item, or to knock on the door with that item. This house is full of love, every corner of it. But there is very little, as I look around, chosen by us, apart from a few potplants, our bed, and a couple of decorative items I have acquired.

Grief, like love, is a universal emotion. Whilst everyone's grief is unique, as is their outward expression of it, it follows a predictable pattern in us all. Shock. Loss of appetite. Difficulty sleeping. Numbness. Denial. Irritability. Anger. Hurt. Sadness. Acceptance.

My own waves of grief, in an outward expression of tears, come at the most unexpected times. And today is no exception. I didn't expect a photo of blue bottles, *my blue bottles,* at my kitchen window, to unleash such an aching loss. Once that hurt hit my chest, I thought I'd never stop crying. The wave engulfed me, threw me, lifted me, and turned me, over and over. And then the wave receded. Perhaps this was my first inkling of the fact that this really happened. That our home is really gone. *Gone.*

When I was a small child, ten or eleven perhaps, my grandfather died. As I recall it, we were not allowed to attend his funeral as perhaps my parents felt it would be too much for my sister and me to handle. I felt inwardly distraught that we had not been invited. I am not sure who initiated it, possibly me, but my memory is that I offered to go and be with my grandmother for some time, to allow her some company and comfort in her time of grief.

Clutching my plane ticket, I boarded the aircraft, feeling small and alone, but determined.

Once in Sydney, with my grandmother, I remember long dark nights lying in the bed next to her as she awoke, in the middle of the night, to cry and cry. In my mind I likened that cry to a wild dog, howling. Primal and raw. I did my best to hold her sobbing body and let her know that somehow, things would be okay...

A friend and neighbour of mine lost her small daughter in a car accident years ago. I was asked to identify the body. At the morgue, the bright lights shone on the girl's tiny bruised body. There was no doubt who the girl was and I was able to positively identify her.

At her funeral, as they lowered her tiny coffin into the earth, her father completely lost control of his emotions and heaving with sobs, called out, 'No, no!' trying physically to jump into his daughter's grave. He had to be restrained. Again, I witnessed that raw, animalistic expression of grief.

Tomorrow is my dear friend John's funeral. It will be very strange that so few will be there to pay their respects. Because of Covid-19 regulations there will only be seven of us at his funeral, and so many that would have attended will be unable to pay their respects and have some closure. Also because of social distancing laws, we in attendance tomorrow won't be able to hug each other. Human touch is a comfort in times of loss, and the first thing I will want to do is give John's wife a hug. But I won't be allowed.

We will be islands in our grief...

We are all, in fact, islands in our grief, whether we grieve the loss of a child, a friend, a relationship, a pet, a home, our health, the environment... yet united in the knowledge that as human beings, loss is something we all must experience.

My friend John Passant's funeral was yesterday. How were any of us ever to imagine that only a maximum of ten people would be allowed to attend? In ordinary, pre-pandemic times, there would have been well over a hundred in attendance...

The breeze blew gently and a mellow sun shone in the clear sky; the only group at the cemetery other than the seven of us gathered, a flock of chattering white cockatoos.

John's brother, a Catholic priest, flew from New Jersey and under Australia's new laws had to go into quarantine for fourteen days. Although unable to see his brother personally to say goodbye, he was able to speak with him over the phone.

As John's wife and two adult children gathered, I felt overwhelmingly the need to hug them. Under the social distancing requirements in place this was not possible, and we stood, a metre or two apart, in our sorrow...

To conclude the service, I sang a poem that John had written, the breeze lifting the words gently into the blue Autumn sky...

Let There Be No Mourning

Let there be no mourning
when tomorrows become today
In that space where the dawning
blasts the grasping past away.

The tired tears the fears display
It is another morning
It is another day.

And we wake not taken
But alive again
to fight to fight my friend
To the end.

                John Passant,
                Songs for the Band Unformed, 2016.

The Great Pause

There is a collective anxiety

The coronavirus pandemic is not only creating fundamental shifts in the way we live, but also in the way we die. All around the country, and indeed the world, funerals are taking place in small groups, or via live-streaming. The human need to come together to mourn and have closure has been denied.

People are creating new and interesting ways to come together whilst distancing is enforced. There are virtual dinner parties taking place on conferencing applications such as *Zoom* which allow a semblance of community in the absence of it. Online music jams, 6pm virtual drinks, pyjama parties and other gatherings created to fuel our need for human contact have arisen.

People are staying indoors, venturing out only for a walk or to buy groceries. There is a surreal quality to life: from having to stand on a red spot taped to the ground in the supermarket, exactly two metres away from the next person; to never seeing a plane in the sky; to knowing that the pleasure of attending the theatre, restaurant, cinema, a concert or a movie, or gathering with friends for a picnic won't be afforded to you anytime soon; to being allowed to buy a take-away cup of coffee but not being allowed to sit on a bench in the park to drink it.

The world is experiencing a new situation that collectively we have never had to deal with before. Travel has come to a standstill.

Flight Centre windows that normally display international airfares are blank and their doors are closed. Supermarket shelves are still empty as people continue panic buying. There is no toilet paper, tissues and cleaning products are scarce, there is a shortage of eggs, jars of pasta sauce and pasta. Before you enter the supermarket you are offered a regulation dollop of hand sanitiser. There are only twenty people allowed into the supermarket at once.

It is late May, Jim and I drive the Hume Highway to Melbourne to pick up his new car, as the Audi TT was recalled for faulty Takata air-bags. The transaction takes place in a busy Motel car park on the intersection of two major highways.

The car is dropped off to us and from it emerge two young men, in their early forties. The transaction is completed and we begin to chat. The men are brothers, and originally from Pakistan. We talk about losing our home, and then about Covid. They both look as though they are holding back tears.

'Our mother died on Friday,' they say gently, their voices heavy with emotion.

'Oh, we are so sorry,' we reply.

'We cannot go to the funeral in Pakistan due to the restrictions of Covid-19...'

The brothers' faces, etched in pain, are illuminated by the bright lamplight on this Melbourne night. Such sorrow, no closure...

Their sad eyes echo in my mind.

There is a collective anxiety because people are unable to plan for their future. No one knows when the pandemic will ease, when restrictions will be loosened, when they will be able to travel again, or even if they will be able to afford to. Yet, there is hope.

From Beijing, photographs are emerging of blue skies above the skyscrapers, for the first time in many years. From Venice, images are appearing of clear blue canals. Even from space, satellite images depict a new, clear, pollution-free atmosphere. And here, in Holt, the skies are so blue, so clear. People talk of seeing an increase in bees and butterflies.

Despite the challenges and hardship, there is hope, that in the stilling of the world and its frantic pace, nature at least will have an opportunity to take a breath and start to heal. Human beings also have the opportunity to still themselves and reflect on what really matters. We are experiencing a collective exhalation.

The Great Pause

Hold tight in this,
The Age of Queen Corona...
We're going in, deeper than we've ever
been called to go before
We're entering the silence
A great white space.
In this seeming blackness
Our strength will be revealed
And we will shine brighter than ever before
For what is a star in the bright light of day?
It is only in the dark black night
that a star shines bright...
We are seeds in the dark earth
Waiting to bloom
This time is our time
To unite
To prepare for evolution
And in revolution
Finally explode from the dark earth
To reach for the yellow sun
As one,

At last,

As one.

Milena Cifali 11 April 2020

Art

'Art enables us to find ourselves and lose ourselves at the same time' – Thomas Merton

The days roll, like waves, one after the other, perfect Autumn days, gentle sunshine kissing our faces and skies an unfurling carpet of never-ending blue. I gaze above, at the infinite sky blue silk parachute, and wonder how, only months ago, smoke clogged the skies and the nostrils, orange and yellow clouds above our heads...

The sky is devoid of aircraft. So still, cloudless.

Most of our days are spent indoors, or on the back veranda, with a few magpies for company.

There is ample time to bake, play music, read, and write.

A package arrives at our front door from Western Australia. The sender is unknown to me. I have been no stranger to unexpected packages at the door in these past weeks.

I take the big box, set it down and continue with my usual activities, glancing every so often at it.

Finally after a couple of days, I decide it's time to reveal its contents. I take a knife and slowly slice through the tape. Opening the box, there are swathes of bubble wrap. Removing it, I find three small paper packages. I tear away the paper to reveal an intricately engraved boab nut, fashioned into a bird. The second and third packages reveal two more carved boab birds. They are exquisite, this bird trio, complete with beaks, eyes, wings and tails.

There is an accompanying note:

> Dear Milena
> I am a friend of your mother, who lives in Kununurra, Western Australia.
> I was so sorry to hear of the loss of your beloved birds and house. I have been meaning to send you these little birds in their memory.
> Making little birds out of boab nuts has been a long tradition in Kununurra. I hope they fly safely to you.
> Love
> Frances

Oh Frances! I don't know you, but what a kind heart you have: to select these birds, wrap them, write this note, and post them to someone you've never met.

I learn that in the Kimberly region of Western Australia, a bottle-shaped boab tree grows, producing nuts from May to September. The nut is used traditionally in various ways: it can be used musically as a maraca, the dry seeds inside creating a percussive sound used to accompany the Corroboree; it can be broken in half and used as a drinking vessel. As a native food source, the inside is rich in Vitamin C, which can be ground to a powder, mixed with water to make a tangy drink. It can be mixed with wild honey and cooked to make a custard. It is also used traditionally as a medicinal supplement for pregnant women. In addition, the seeds can be roasted and eaten like peanuts.

Traditionally, women gather to pick the nuts together, either from the ground or straight from the tree. Nuts picked in June or July, Australian winter, are the best for carving, as these have the lowest water content.

The carving process begins by removing the furry green coating. Tools utilised include razor blades, pocket knives, bits of tin cans and commercial sharpening tools.

The trio of birds that have flown to us are each engraved by a different Aboriginal artist: Maureen Simon, Muriel Wildbelee, and Yvonne Doondoognun.

I wonder if these women realize how far their little carved birds have flown to help us in our healing. They say:

'Ngenjayinga dawanga ngoodnenintha
Birrgamib-gerring Ngoondengig yirremandayin
Ngenjaying dawang Miriwoong Yawwrroobtha
Yirrb yirrowindayin warrgeb-gerring
Woomgib-gerring, birrgamib-gerring.'

'It's a good art centre-this place.
We respect and do good things in this Miriwoong country.
We all come together here to dance and sing
And make things.'

Thank you for these things.

Art. A wall without art is merely a wall. A wall hung with art speaks, creates beauty, or statements, or questions; it makes a house a home.

I relish creating art and my medium is music. Yet I also love to draw with soft pastels, creating layer upon layer of colourful expression.

One of our bedrooms in this new house has become my granddaughter Willow's room. It has a bed, her bed, a lamp, a dream catcher and a sign which reads 'Willow's Room'.

Yesterday we opened the box of coloured pastels which I bought myself after I lost all of mine, along with my sketch pad full of accompanying artworks. A new clean white sheet of paper lay before us, the rows of colours waiting patiently to meet the page.

Willow selected a violet pastel, and her two year old fingers holding it carefully, slowly pushed the flat end across the page, leaving a large violet streak on the white paper. Her face a study in concentration, she picked a dark forest green and made a big circle over the top, the violet and the green melding in places to create a new, unnamed colour.

Sunshine yellow followed, creating lime green over forest green. Her eyes shining with wonder, she continued to push, slide, swirl and streak the page with her colourful marks, declaring finally, 'It's finished'.

'Let's hang it in your bedroom,' I said.

And in that moment, with the placing of art, her art, on the wall, the bedroom became her bedroom, a place of life, of expression.

We have been blessed beyond belief since arriving here in Canberra to have received the artistic offerings our artist friends have been thoughtful enough to gift us. Our shelves and walls are adorned with their creations of love.

A friend from Mallacoota paints us a miniature on a tiny wooden easel, of the bush around Mallacoota regenerating with new green life, a stark contrast against the blackened wood. The painting symbolises new hope and our friend Jeanette passes some of this hope along to us by sending us her little masterpiece.

Another friend, Philippa, whose medium is block print, knocks on the door one day with one of her framed prints, in blues, browns and purples, of a gypsy cart with a horse, and a gypsy couple playing guitar under a starry night sky. The man is bearded and the woman has long hair. The painting represents myself and Jim, travelling the countryside playing our music. It is beautiful and I am deeply touched. The wall in our lounge room is transformed with its hanging.

Another dear friend, Linda, sends us a gift for our housewarming party which she is unable to attend. Hand-painted budgerigars, flashes of electric blue, yellow and green, flying amidst a flowering eucalypt. We instantly fall in love with it. It hangs on another wall in our lounge room, and reminds us of our friend Linda.

Another prolific and talented artist friend whom we met travelling back from Brisbane to Canberra, Beth Croudace, had invited us to her home to select a painting to auction on her behalf, her wish being that proceeds would go to wildlife affected by bush fires.

Whilst at her place, she was generous enough to gift us a beautiful painting of a duck, and also, at a later stage, mailed us a framed watercolour of Jim with our beloved parrot Blossom on his shoulder. We are humbled at her generosity and the duck now hangs in the dining room, watching us have dinner each evening at our round table.

Our friend Pamela gifts us a joyful musical painting of animals dancing, playing cellos and trumpets. It makes me want to dance also. I hang it above our bed.

Our dear friend Leanne, who looked after our beautiful birds every time we were away from Mallacoota, has the very special gift of knitting birds. Her birds are in galleries far and wide, and are character-filled replicas of magpies, lyrebirds, seagulls, lorikeets and any other birds that she feels drawn to knit. She handed us a bag with a wrapped gift in it as we left Mallacoota to return to Canberra after seeing the ash pile that was once our home.

At home, we unwrapped the contents. There, in wool, sat our Blossom and Winston, bead eyes looking at us so expressively as to momentarily stop us in our tracks. Blossom and Winston live in the kitchen of this new house, and are a poignant reminder of our love for our feathered family members who so tragically perished. They live in our hearts forever.

To all our artist friends, *thank you...*

These are the building blocks that reassemble my soul, the day it fragmented and turned to ash...

MUSIC

'After silence, that which comes nearest to expressing the inexpressible is music'–Aldous Huxley

After we had been in the house in Holt for several weeks I decided to hold a housewarming party. My idea was that we open the house all day to our friends, and offer them home-cooked curries and an opportunity for us all to connect.

I did not realise how many of our friends are musicians. From the moment our front door opened, until it shut ten hours later, the house was filled with spontaneous and joyful music. We glided from Jazz to Blues, Latin to Flamenco to Bossa Nova. There was the sweet tone of the flute, the syrupy sigh of the saxophone, velvety electric bass, cheerful mandolin, African *djembe*, Middle-Eastern *darbuka*, classical guitar, twelve-string guitar, male voices, female voices, hands clapping, feet tapping... and there was our big bowl of percussion instruments that had turned up on our doorstep one day, being put to use—clapping sticks, maracas, shakers, eggs, tambourine, bells...

The walls and floor absorbed our collective music-making all day, and that night as the house emptied and we cleaned up, we could still hear the music reverberating in our hearts: the house felt *warmed*.

Because of the Covid-19 restrictions music performances and festivals all over Australia have been cancelled. The National Folk Festival, held over Easter each year, has been shut down. The Cobargo Folk Festival, cancelled. The fortieth anniversary of the

Merimbula Jazz Festival, at which we were looking forward to performing, cancelled. This is just in Australia. Worldwide, the music industry has been affected by coronavirus. Massively popular festivals such as the Glastonbury and Montreaux Jazz festivals have been cancelled. Musicians, sound engineers, recording studios, booking agents and managers, event staff, and roadies are all impacted. The music industry has been brought to its knees.

There is some speculation that certain restrictions may begin to be loosened over the coming weeks but music and music festivals are not amongst them. Realistically, no music festival can be expected to take place for at least the remainder of this year and, from some accounts, possibly longer.

So, people have found new ways, using technology, to host online music festivals. Entire choirs have come together virtually to sing together online. With constraints on the movements of societies, people are collectively feeling a loss of control and an anxiety about what the future holds. Music provides a way to unite, to regain control and to lessen anxiety. In Italy, during the peak of the lockdown, Italians were emerging on their balconies, to sing together in one voice, uniting each other in their time of isolation. In Spain also, footage has emerged of people making music together across apartment buildings. In Barcelona, a pianist performed ' My Heart Will go On ' from his balcony. Shortly after, a saxophonist in the building next door to his began accompanying him.

In Wuhan, China, citizens in quarantine sing patriotic songs from their windows, boosting each other's morale.

Music is a way of knocking down the barriers of isolation and alienation that have been thrust upon the world since March 2020. These barriers have created panic and uncertainty. Music is the antidote, providing connection in a time of disconnection. Humanity and music go hand in hand and now more than ever in these uncertain and surreal times, the importance of music on humanity is not lost.

In Mallacoota, the community was a musical one. There were always regular get-togethers where people sang and strummed together. After the bush fires, with the collective trauma that communities such as that of Mallcoota suffered, music making was a way to come together and express emotion without necessarily having to say a word.

All around Australia during the height of the bushfire season, concerts large and small were organised to raise funds for fire-ravaged communities.

In the Mallacoota fire, we lost ten guitars, three basses, a drum kit, a mandolin, a saxophone, a keyboard, percussion instruments, a *darbuka* from Alexandria—my parents birthplace—a clarinet, a violin, and musical accessories: metronomes, capos, guitar tuners, music stands. And music! My own hand-written music, composed lovingly, painstakingly. A lifetime collection of guitar music and books. CDs. Our entire library of music CDs of artists that we enjoy and love, as well as all the CDs that we have recorded ourselves over the years, of our own work... so many sounds, thousands upon thousands of notes, so many musical memories, consumed, in one moment, by fire.

All these are irreplaceable. But we are alive! We have been donated guitars, mandolins, and violins. We can write, perform and record more music, collaborate with other musicians, acquire more music

to listen to, and if we wish, we can go out on our own balcony, and sing! We can sing away the bushfires, sing away the coronavirus, sing away our heartache, sing away the homesickness, sing away, as humanity has done for aeons before us, and will continue to do long after we ourselves have silently been laid to rest...

The Full Moon Cafe

*And if you weren't there
you weren't there*

In Alice Springs, where my children were born in the late eighties, there existed a house by the edge of the dry sandy bed of the Todd River, known as The Full Moon Cafe. As a young mother of two small children, and wanting to connect with others musically, I would go, once a month on the full moon, to The Full Moon Cafe, guitar and babies in tow, to see what offerings life would throw at me.

Each event was a complete unknown; travelling musicians, artists, poets, puppeteers, sculptors and writers would arrive from interstate or overseas.

Deliciously impulsive collisions of expression would occur, uplifting and delighting the senses. A collection of tribal drums, arranged in a circle under the heavy circle of the full moon, a fire flickering nearby offering comfort and warmth. Puppets and brightly clothed people dancing to the rise and fall of the drumming. Fire twirlers, a visiting cellist or saxophonist contributing to the collective energy... An event always pregnant with possibility, like the full moon above.

Music, always music. Returning to The Full Moon Cafe was returning home.

Full Moon Cafe

The old house was the scene for the full moon cafe
The eucalypts shone in the light of the moon
The world was your oyster
your dreams became real
at the full moon cafe

You could be anyone
you wanted to be
at the full moon cafe
Your biggest ambition
was just to be there
at the full moon cafe
at the full moon cafe

And if you weren't there
you weren't there
And if you didn't know about it
you didn't know about it
But if you do
then lucky you then lucky you

The people you met
at the full moon cafe
we are precious and rare and the air was so cool
and the coffee so hot
and the pot belly stove burnt on through the night and the wine and the song
flowed on through the night
And everything was always alright yes everything was always alright
And if you weren't there
you weren't there

And if you didn't know about it
you didn't know about it
but if you do
then lucky you
at the full moon cafe
at the full moon cafe
at the full moon cafe

For Sean Peter Verdon

The Never-Ending Chai

A little magic

Jim and I are arguing. It becomes a part of our daily routine, squabbling like hungry seagulls. We argue about where the teaspoon went, and why the guitar was put back on the stand at this or that angle. Small issues become big ones.

This is a by-product of our situation, of being together every moment in this house, in a new environment, in isolation, following coronavirus restrictions, and also suffering residual trauma from the bushfires, which everyone seems to have forgotten about.

A friend came to visit yesterday, who owns a property near fire-ravaged Cobargo, NSW. He says that twenty close friends of his have lost their homes. Twenty!

'Everyone knows someone who has lost their home,' he says.

We also talk about a mutual friend who has lost her brother in the fires. I try and imagine losing a family member in the fires and shudder. Too intense a thought to contemplate...

Queen Corona has stolen the limelight. People are dying each day in numbers too huge to contemplate. In America, as of the 20 April 2020, 'usatoday.com' reports that the death toll has reached 40,000, with over 746,000 cases in the U.S. and 2.4 million cases worldwide, with 165, 000 deaths globally.

We have been appointed a caseworker to help us navigate through these tumultuous times and he has proven to be our anchor in these rough waters.

Neville calls today to see how we are coping. I explain that we are bickering frequently over small nothings, and at the crux of this, I believe, is the fact that we can't really move forward as we don't have a clear direction in place, as life is on hold, uncertainty looming for us all...

I say, 'I have made my mind up about one thing though.'

'What's that?' he asks.

'I can't go back to Mallacoota,' and with that, I start to sob, heaving sobs of deep grief.

I take myself, and him, by surprise. It is the first time I have articulated these words: *I can't go back to Mallacoota...*

Mallacoota, one of the most beautiful, magical chapters of my life so far; Mallacoota, of beauty so profound it left me thunderstruck; Mallacoota, where we were surrounded each day by a parade of wildlife that we loved, and that trusted us; Mallacoota, where our little cedar cottage was our safe haven, and where the light in the trees in the late afternoon made me feel that all was right with the world...

To go back would mean accepting that either there would never be another bushfire, an unrealistic likelihood, or that if there were another bushfire, that we might have to go through the nightmare of losing yet another home, a more realistic outcome, and one I am not prepared to go through. Beyond that, precisely because that chapter of our lives was so... perfect, there is no way that I can rewrite that chapter in Mallacoota. I simply can't and don't wish to attempt to replicate that perfection. I will take a fresh sheet, blank with possibilities,and write a brand new chapter, full of promise, in a new location.

In the meantime, we wait, in Canberra, our lives narrowed to a family of four magpies who visit twice a day, four possums who visit at sundown for their breakfast (yes, it is the first meal of their day, as they awake at sunset), some guitar playing, Saturdays with Willow, cups of tea, a meal together, a stroll to the ridge behind our place to watch the sun sink over the Brindabellas turning them purple blue and washing the sky pink... and arising to a new day, once again, to do more of the same.

Jim and I met in Bermagui on the 8th of October 2011. He was fifty-six and I was forty-six.

Interestingly, we both arrived in Australia on ships in the same year, 1966, and the same month, May; Jim from Novi Sad in the former Yugoslavia and I from the Port of Genoa in Italy. He disembarked with his family in Melbourne, and I with mine in Sydney.

It was online, in 2011, that our journey began. We began conversing and discovered a mutual connection through music.

After several weeks we decided to meet in Bermagui, which was roughly halfway between Canberra, where I resided, and Kiah, near Eden, NSW, where Jim resided.

We had agreed to meet at The River Rock Cafe in Bermagui at around midday. On that day, I spoke on the phone to a friend of mine and explained that I was going to meet a man I had known for some time online, in Bermagui, and that if I wasn't back within twenty-four hours to send out a search party.

We had agreed that when we met, we would not speak any words to begin with; that I would arrive to meet him and the first thing I would do was to sing a song.

I arrived on that sunny October day, with a few knots in my stomach, which dissolved when I saw Jim. I felt that I knew him, straight away. He greeted me with a very open, genuine smile, and I sat down and opened my guitar case, and began to sing:

'I heard there was a secret chord, ...
Hallelujah, Hallelujah...'

A single tear rolled down Jim's cheek. We went inside, and ordered a pot of chai.

We talked, walked, laughed, and the afternoon turned to night...

I wrote a piece shortly after we met:

> Yes, I'm lonely. Never alone, but always lonely. I sleep alone, and don't bother to eat. Some of those observing me during this time say I'm depressed.
>
> Depressed or not, something needs to change. So it is that on this chilly September morning I tentatively log on to a dating website.
>
> As I plough through the profiles of so many strangers, I feel as though I'm strolling through the cereal aisle of a supermarket, trying to choose my breakfast.
>
> Although this, this is far more important than breakfast. If indeed I find a stranger who appeals, my world could literally be rearranged in the blink of an eye.
>
> After wading through endless profiles of conservative men who enjoy 'wining, dining, movies and sunset walks,' I'm starting to feel jaded. There seems nothing inspiring in this world of cyber strangers.
>
> Then it happens. I chance upon a picture of a man, sitting near the river, with two blue-eyed children and a dog.

His eyes, his face, his soul. I can't draw my eyes away! A stranger perhaps, but like a bolt out of the blue I feel I know him. My heart leaps to my throat as I hit 'chat request'. There's no going back.

A chat online turns to a phone call.

His voice deep, gravelly, laying bare all truths. He stands naked before me, no stone unturned. I like him.

I suggest we meet. Halfway. For coffee. At the River Rock Cafe. Yes. He agrees.

So there I am on that sunny October morning, driving to meet the stranger, my heart beating at the possibilities.

We've agreed that we won't speak at first, that I'll approach him with my guitar and sing him a song. 'Which song?' I've asked him. 'Go with the flow,' has been his reply.

I arrive and see him there, waiting outside the cafe. He smiles at me and at that moment he's no stranger. I know his eyes, his smile. In a flash my world is rearranged. We walk as though in slow motion to a bench outside the cafe. I take out my guitar, and begin to sing:

'I heard there was a secret chord, ...'

Hallelujah.

He listens, entranced and I see a single tear roll down his cheek. Inside we drink chai, not coffee but chai.

We talk walk laugh sing drive sleep wake smile. A day becomes a week becomes a month becomes a year.

Together we travel far and wide and play music. We buy a cottage near the sea and feed the wild birds and walk on the beach.

I sing for him, 'Sail away with me honey, put my heart in your hands.' I give him a small heart made of cool green jade to keep in his pocket. And he does.

We marvel at the chance of our online rendezvous and at the wonder of life when it throws us a little magic.

That night turned into another, and another. I called my friend and explained that I had fallen in love...

Bermagui Sun

So we met for a pot of chai,
both tired of life passing us by,
said we'd meet about halfway,
a quarter past twelve at The River Rock Cafe.
I met your eyes, I knew them well,
and when you smiled, well, I could tell,
That smile would turn the rain to sun,
that smile would make me come undone.
So we talked about life for a while,
And then we walked down the road for a couple of miles,
From Wallaga Lake to the top of the hill,
And there we stood and time stood still,
It was there you shared with me your pain,
It was there you smiled at me again.
That smile could turn the rain to sun,
That smile would make me come undone,
That smile would make me come undone,
Under the Bermagui sun,
oh yes, that smile would make me come undone.

For the first year or two, Jim and I were truly gypsies. I left behind my house and life in Canberra, feeling the need to shed my skin, to travel and sing.

And travel and sing we did. We played music wherever and whenever we could.

In those early days, Jim only knew four or five songs on the bass, so we would just busk, or play on the balcony of an old country hotel.

In his earlier life, Jim had been a drummer and drummed with the famous Australian blues band Chain. In his teenage years his tutor had been Stewie Speer from Max Merrit and the Meteors.

In 1986, Jim had been riding a motorbike with a pillion passenger on the back, and at Melbourne's Beaconsfield Parade, in St Kilda, they had been cut off by a vehicle at the intersection and hit the median strip.

What followed was eighteen months in hospital, with eighty-five percent of the bones in Jim's body broken. Sadly, the pillion passenger, Les, died. Upon arrival at hospital, Jim died clinically, and had to be revived due to blood loss. He suffered broken ribs, pelvis, shoulder and scapula, wrist and finger, underwent an artery bypass, two hip replacements, two knee replacements, countless skin grafts on his legs, and was informed that he would need his leg amputated. A month later, he became depressed at the thought of spending the rest of his days in hospital, unable to move, totally suspended in framework, with tubes and drains embedded in his body. He ripped out his life support system, effectively cutting off the oxygen to his brain. This was the second time he died clinically.

As Jim explains the experience, 'There are a lot of happenings and unmapped places out there when you die. Life just doesn't end when your heart stops beating. You travel out into the infinity of space and time. There is no navigation system out there ...'

Being a rebel at heart, as soon as he was well enough to sit up, Jim would escape the hospital in his wheelchair to the Station Hotel in Gravel Street Prahran, until the nurses ordered for him to be returned to the Hospital. Jim then started escaping in his wheelchair, eight kilometres or so, to The Esplanade Hotel in St Kilda, with only a towel draped over his lap, and a t-shirt, as his clothes had been confiscated by the nurses.

It was at The Esplanade Hotel one afternoon, on one of his escapades, that Jim was talking to some friends, telling them about the surgeons insisting on amputating his leg. A man with a bushy beard and long salt and pepper hair approached Jim and said that he couldn't help but overhear the conversation. The man, an orthapaedic surgeon, said that if Jim was interested, and prepared to sign a waiver verified by two witnesses, he would look into Jim's medical files and see if there was something he could do to help to save his leg. Jim gave him the benefit of the doubt, even though as Jim puts it, 'He didn't look like any surgeon I have ever met before.'

Three days later Jim received a call at his bedside in hospital. It was the bearded surgeon from the Esplanade. He introduced himself as Bill Donohue and went on to tell Jim that he'd had a look at the files and believed that he could save his leg.

He promptly booked Jim a bed at the Southern Memorial Hospital in Caulfield. With the assistance of his father, Jim moved to the new hospital and shortly afterwards underwent successful surgery to retain his limb.

Jim had to learn to walk again and undergo extensive rehabilitation. He found the process uninspiring, so decided to conduct his own rehabilitation by playing pool. This involved playing in his wheelchair for the first few months, and then learning to lift himself out of the wheelchair with the use of the pool cue and the edge of the table. Gradually, he was able to gain strength, but remained wheelchair bound for over a year.

Prior to the accident in 1986, Jim had been a very competent athlete, and passionate surfer, surfing the West Coast of Victoria, following the surf wherever it was.

He had also been a competitive gymnast—third in Australia in the junior category—as well as being a tower and springboard diver. He was a competitive speed skater—also placing third in Australia—and a very competent skier. To have lost the use of his limbs and mobility so suddenly, as a very fit and active man in his prime at the age of thirty, was a tremendous blow to have to adjust to.

When I had spoken to Jim on the phone, before I met him, I remember him saying, 'My legs aren't pretty.' I admired his honesty.

Days turned to weeks and Jim and I were inseparable. We called our pot of chai 'The Never-Ending Chai'.

We could never have imagined that eight years after we met, our home would be destroyed by fire...

And now, it seems that our life together has collapsed into one which has become introverted and narrowed; before the fire and before the Covid-19 pandemic the world felt like it was ours for the taking, and take it we did. We performed music festivals, roamed magnificent beaches, slept in magical forests, met endless characters from all walks of life on our travels. These days were ours for the taking...

Ours for the Taking

You went for a walk the other night,
Sitting there alone in the dark,
A thought occurred razor sharp,
what if you didn't come back?
What on earth would I do,
I'd be one instead of a solid two,
I'd find it hard to keep on singing,
I'd have to go back to the very beginning.
Start my life back at square one,
But would I feel the shining sun,
Would I smell the summer air,
Would I even care?
Would I hear the singing birds?
Would I watch the sparkling sea?
If you were not sitting close,
To watch it all with me?

I suppose what I'm saying is you're my anchor,
I suppose what I'm saying is you're my harbour,
I suppose what I'm saying is thank you,
I suppose what I'm saying is I love you,
These are our memories in the making,
These are our days, ours for the taking,
This is our endless road to travel,
This is our mystery to unravel...

The Lost Summer

...ocean waves were blackened

It is Autumn in Canberra. The change in season is magical. Autumn is a magnificent lady, resplendent in ruby, amber and claret. I drink in the clear blue sky, the mellow midday sun on my skin, the crisp chill of the evening, when the sky turns palest pink.

Rains have arrived, kissing the country green. All is beautiful.

But globally, over 200,000 have succumbed to Covid-19, and in the United States, over 50,000. Its President, Donald Trump, has bizarrely suggested that the virus could be cured by injecting disinfectant into the body and lungs. The world has become more surreal by the moment.

Against this backdrop, we wait, uncertainty looming over our heads.

Today I experienced anxiety and agitation. I feel tension at the idea of leaving this house. I do not want to leave again. I do not want to leave this house. I cannot bear the idea of packing and moving.

I feel anchored, here in this lovely house, but in reality I am anchorless. I do not know where we will go, or what we will do. I am entertaining the idea of buying this house, perhaps making it *home*. I am contemplating the idea of moving North, being near the ocean again. I just don't know. I am tired of not knowing. Time is ticking, ticking, dripping, eroding. I want to be in the present because here, now, all is well. We have food in our fridge, instruments in our loungeroom, artwork on the walls, and a warm bed. We have the joy of the autumn days rolling out before us. The present is safe. As soon as I begin to think about the future, the unknown, my breath quickens. Should we stay in Canberra? Move North? South, to the ocean?

I miss the ocean. The beach is a two-hour drive from Canberra but people are not able to travel with current restrictions. No one knows how long they will last. The ocean is so near, yet so far.

As a child growing up in Canberra, like so many others most of our holidays and summers were spent at the beach. There was the interminable drive to Braidwood—'are we there yet?'—then mounting excitement as we passed Braidwood, the poplars along each side of the road ushering us through towards the freedom of salt air and lazy sandy days, and then the slow, winding descent down the Clyde Mountain.

Poplar Road

Ever since I was a little child,
Wheels rolling down Poplar Road,
Carried me to the ocean, carried me to be free
And as the years roll by
it carries me still,
like it always did and it always will...
Poplar Road,

carries me to the ocean
Poplar Road, carries me to the sea,
Poplar road, carries me to the ocean,
Poplar Road, carries me to be free...

The past eight years have been spent skirting the coastline, both in Mallacoota and along the South Coast as we have travelled playing music.

From our cottage in Mallacoota, it was an eight-minute stroll to the vast expanse of Bastion Beach. We would stand on the cliff and watch the ebb and flow of turquoise, aqua, emerald and sapphire, before meandering down the stairs past tea tree scrub to the golden sweep of sand.

We would feel small under the massive expanse of Mallacoota skies, with the ocean rolling out to the horizon.

We would walk northwards, half an hour or so, to the entrance, where the river meets the sea. We felt like we were walking to the edge of the earth. And indeed we were...

The powerful forces of the elements changed the beachscape endlessly. The curve and flow of the water running out to sea, the rippled sandbanks there one day, gone the next.

The mood of the sea and sky were also ever-changing. There were golden aqua days, breezy and bright, oppressively hot; still days where the light was intense and the sea seemed sluggish; wild windy black and grey days, the sea churning and white, the air slapping our faces with salt spray; wintry crisp white and blue days, cold and sparkling; gentle silvery violet days, whispering sweet nothings. There were late afternoons—or were they early evenings—the silver sea gradually awash in watercolour pinks, reflecting the dusk rose clouds above... Mallacoota nights sometimes brought us the joy of a moonrise over the bay, viewed from the cliff. I have never seen or *felt* the moon so keenly as when we experienced it in Mallacoota, golds and silvers shining off the black waters.

These ocean walks were *ours*. The beach was often empty. We marvelled at the proximity and the beauty. We were thunderstruck. We thought these days would last forever.

The bushfires of Summer 2020 devastated the South Coast. Townships all along the coast were evacuated once, twice, three times, towns we knew and loved, where we had friends and knew each beach, each cafe. Towns where we had shared our music: Bermagui, Cobargo, Narooma, Malua Bay, Moruya, Tilba, Batemans Bay, Ulladulla, Sussex Inlet, and beyond. Photographs showed terrifying smoke and red skies, over and over, all summer. People became stressed, shell-shocked, exhausted. Everyone was affected, or knew someone who was affected. Homes were lost, lives were lost, businesses closed. People stopped travelling, or travelled only on evacuation orders.

The ocean waves were blackened, with reports of beach after beach of washed-up ash. It was a Lost Summer, in stark contrast to the carefree beach days of summers past.

When the last fires eventually burnt out, people celebrated. It was time to go and visit these coastal towns, buy fish and chips, have surfing lessons, drink coffee and buy local produce, stay at local hotels. Summer may have been lost, but Autumn would bring recovery.

Covid-19 put a sudden stop to that. Now, beaches are deserted. All along the coast, the story repeats itself: tourist towns, such as heritage-listed Tilba, now ghost towns. Businesses shut. Seagulls hungry—where are the chips? Pubs, clubs, and breweries which echoed with laughter and live music, silent. Hotels, motels, and caravan parks, empty.

I yearn to go back to the ocean, dip my toes in the foamy waves, feel the sand under my feet, and share a few chips with the gulls.

But even that is an unknown.

Meanwhile, I will dream of Mallacoota's magical beach offerings and treasure my memories of enchanted moments, at one with nature, as I so often was, before we wandered back home to our little cottage with sandy feet to sit on our balcony with a cup of tea and bask in the afternoon light, while the sound of the waves caressed our souls.

FRIENDS

Beauty... at every turn

And then, there was the lake; the inlet estuary consisting of Top Lake and Bottom Lake. The vast, silvery expanse of water named Mallacoota Inlet, where the Genoa and Wallagaraugh Rivers flow into The Narrows, finally opening out into the magnificent spread of water that flows out to Bass Strait.

Bordered by the wilderness of the Croajingolong National Park, the inlet attracts colonies of black swans, the ubiquitous pelicans, sea-eagles, all types of fish, and seals.

The mood of the lake alters many times a day, with the ever-changing light, and whispers its stories for all who listen.

We camped, with Jim's children, by the lake in the tourist park for a week or so, and we were able to flow with the rhythms of the lake, with its early morning mirror-like calmness, its choppy mid-afternoon breeziness, its evening serenity, washed silver pink, its night-time blackness, its midnight secrets...

We took a sailing trip with our friend Tony, on his small wooden yacht, and let the wind carry us outwards, past small sandy islands, the lake breezes fresh and uplifting.

When I noticed water trickling, then flooding in, I alerted Tony and Jim, and with a bucket, we began to bail ferociously, trying to keep the water out. The trip ended safely, although I had mentally prepared myself for a cold swim back to dry land. It was an exhilarating bonding with the waters of the Inlet.

Driving home from wherever we had been on our travels, we would always take the scenic route, winding our way into Mallacoota via the lake and following Lakeside Drive into the township.

Each and every time we returned, we would look at each other, thunderstruck, when greeted with the magnificence of the enormous waterway, framed by the watercolour blues of the Howe Ranges in the distance.

Beauty, it seemed, surrounded us at every turn, in our Mallacoota time...

Along with beauty, there were friendships forged in Mallacoota, or strengthened there.

Our door was always open to all, and we delighted in sharing our home, our food, and our music with others.

One day, I read a notice on a noticeboard: a couple were desperately seeking accommodation over the Christmas period and had no success. They were offering a house swap in Melbourne in return for accommodation in Mallacoota.

I made contact with them and suggested they might like to join us for Christmas.

'It's a small cottage but you're most welcome to come and stay with us.'

The couple, Maria and Lorem, and their young daughter, Nawa, took us up on the offer. We were to share our home and Christmas with total strangers.

Maria was Spanish, and Lorem Brazilian. We decided to have a shared Christmas. I cooked seafood salad and spaghetti with prawns, and Maria concocted a delectable Spanish custard flan with homemade chocolate ice-cream. Lorem played the Berimbau, a traditional Brazilian instrument used in the dynamic dance-like martial art known as *Capoeira*, and Jim and I performed Brazilian Bossa Nova for our new friends. This turned out to be one of our most enjoyable, spontaneous and memorable Christmas celebrations ever, and we became firm friends, little Nawa becoming like a granddaughter to us... We would visit them whenever we were in Melbourne. Taking that leap to invite total strangers to share our home was serendipitous, leading to a lifelong bond.

I invited our bird carer friend Leanne and her son around for dinner once every three weeks or so. I would create international dishes, travelling around the world through cuisine. These nights left beautiful happy memories, of Vietnamese, French, Thai, Italian, Egyptian, Malaysian, Russian and Hungarian dinners, with poetry, music, and general knowledge and even special outfits to complement the occasion.

There were visits from friends in Canberra, some alone, some with partners, some with two or four children in tow. We made them feel welcome and comfortable, and they all left spellbound by Mallacoota's charms...

There was always music: sometimes jazz, sometimes blues, sometimes folk, always shared.

The house soaked up all these connections—the laughter, the music—and exuded warmth.

Amidst the joys of friendship and music, there were a couple of notably strange episodes. There were several occasions where we needed a house-sitter, if we were to be away longer than six weeks. There were three house-sitters in total and two of them proved wonderful. The third, not so...

I asked a friend in Canberra, who was a bird and animal lover, if he would be interested, and he accepted.

He was in Mallacoota for six weeks or so. Upon notifying him of our return, he inexplicably decided to leave before we arrived. We entered our home, and like a scene from a surreal movie, all our furniture had been moved around. Everything had changed: paintings were hung in different positions, the table had shifted, even spice jars on the kitchen bench had been put away inside cupboards. He had moved things outside, such as rock and shell collections, and even, bizarrely, pulled apart earrings that belonged to me and crafted hanging mobiles out of them. The bird cage which housed Blossom and Winston was outside, with them in it. We had no idea how long it had been out there. Needless to say, that was the final time we ever had a house-sitter stay in Mallacoota...

When the poet John Passant came to Mallacoota for our book and CD launch, we performed a house concert at Don Ashby's place. Performing with us were our friends and their partners: a harp player from Tilba, Michael, a trombone player, Max and percussionist Robbie Beel from Orbost. Afterwards, I invited the musicians back to our place for dinner. Spontaneously, after dinner, a music jam began... it was wild, loud, free, and unreservedly joyful. It reminded me of gypsy flamenco music crossed with African tribal rhythms. We banged, blew, strummed and vocalised into the night, our faces beaming with happiness, our little cottage bursting with passion...

That night, and many more like it, sum up for me what our Mallacoota home was all about.

And amidst the ash and the rubble, the notes and the laughter live on still...

Memories

Poignant Mallacoota memories
nurtured forever in safe corners of my heart...

My father, Guido, making a special journey from Brisbane to Mallacoota to share my fiftieth birthday with me. A geologist, and a nature lover, marvelling at the many splendid rock formations on Mallacoota's pristine beaches. Walking together on the beach, and stopping in an ancient cave, father and daughter singing harmonies, time standing still, with only the crashing waves accompanying our song on the wild and empty beach...

Jim and Milena, newcomers to Mallacoota, on the enormous empty beach, alone, under the great expanse of sky, writing our names in the sand, *Jim and Milena*, claiming it as ours...

January 17, 2014, a full moon night…

My eldest son called me, sobbing, to inform me that his father had died. It was a hot midsummer's Mallacoota night. South Australia had experienced several days of heatwave conditions with temperatures approaching the mid forties. My son's father, Merv, was found slumped against a tree in a park, deceased. He was fifty-three.

I was consumed by intense grief, and that night I went to stand on the clifftop overlooking the ocean to watch the moon rise and think of Merv. Merv was always a lover of the moon and its cycles, and it seemed tonight it was rising in his memory, larger, fuller, brighter than I could ever recall any full moon…

I returned home and wrote a song:

Mallacoota Moon

Tonight's blood moon is on the rise
Over a world that's gone insane
but you're standing here beside me
so I guess things will be okay
looking out over the black ocean
waves of fear start to spread
but there's a mellow Mallacoota moon rising
and it's lighting the dolphins way
moon rise over ocean
moon shine over sea
moon rise over ocean
feels good to me.
Mellow Mallacoota moon rising
Mellow Mallacoota moon rising...

A meteorite, lighting up the sky in a blinding three-second flash of brilliant turquoise-aqua, as though an entire fireworks display was happening in my garden. My Mallacoota meteorite, crashing into the atmosphere, radiantly seared in my memory forever...

When I was gifted this painting by my friend Carolyn Kidd, I was floored.

There was my Mallacoota, in the fiery orange sky, in the browned tea tree scrub. And in the brilliant blue flashes that seared the orange sky, I rediscovered my Mallacoota meteorite.

The painting now graces our wall in our Canberra home, and I have hung it strategically so that when I arise each morning, it is the first thing my eyes see. Each day, I am floored again with the intensity of this painting, and its direct connection in my soul with Mallacoota.

MOVING

... something I have no wish to do again

Today Jim went to Mallacoota. He has been wanting to do so for a long time. For him, it is very important to go and sift through the rubble and see if he can find any remnants: maybe my grandmother's brass crocodile nutcracker, maybe an old tool that Jim's father once held in his hands, perhaps the little cross that I bought at the Vatican. Perhaps he will find nothing, other than a sense of closure. And perhaps not even that...

We are all different, responding uniquely to situations we are presented with in life. Personally, I have no desire whatsoever to rummage through ash, and indeed, have a specific desire to stay well away. As for the stuff that may or may not lie under the rubble, I couldn't care less. I have let it all go. I have surrendered... If Jim could bring back our beloved birds, alive and well, now that would be another matter...

Each day I am plagued by tumultuous feelings which are in conflict with each other; I want to nest, to enter this space fully, to enjoy each day as it arises. Simultaneously, I dread leaving this house and so am trying to disassociate myself from it, in readiness for what appears to be our inevitable departure.

I have moved many times in my life. It is something I have no wish to do again.

When I started high school at that awkward pre-teen stage in 1977, we were living with my family in Canberra and had just moved from a small red brick cottage in the inner south suburb of Deakin, to a very large and rambling mansion in Garran. Coupled with this, I was just on the threshold of puberty, and grappling with high school, which was a foreign and unknown environment. My first year there was unhappy. I was often in trouble, unable to fit in with school friends, who were much more 'Australian' than I was, having grown up in a European household.

One day, it was announced that we were moving to Iran. And just like that, or so it seemed, I was dropped into a new environment, going from an Australian High School where I was too European, to a British-Iranian High School in Tehran, where I couldn't fit in because I was too Australian.

I had entered a whole new world. A world of mosques, prayer rugs, and tea served black in small glasses with two lumps of sugar from a *Samovar*. A world where women crouched by the deep gutters, washing their clothes in the clear water that ran down them from cold mountain streams. A world where men sat on one side of the room and women, in their black *chadors*, on the other. A world where the *muzaneen* woke me at 5am every morning from the loudspeaker that faced our kitchen window. A world of pungent spice bazaars,

of hot roasted corn on the cob or beetroot, eaten standing at a street stall, of fragrant rosewater ice-cream enjoyed as we strolled through the snow, a world where to be thirteen and a foreigner meant you could not walk outside without being whistled at, followed, or harassed.

The year was 1978. The Iranian Revolution was playing out before my impressionable young eyes. Being thirteen, I was not interested in the politics of the situation, whose goal was the overthrow of the Pahlavi Dynasty, caused by mounting discontent with the Shah's rule, and which culminated with Ayatollah Ruhollah Khomeini becoming the new Supreme Leader of Iran. As the year progressed, Martial Law was introduced, and through my thirteen-year-old eyes I saw tanks, with armed soldiers, on each corner. They were just part of the scenery. At some stage in that year, a curfew was introduced, and I clearly recall the absolute terror of driving home across the city, knowing that the 9pm deadline to be indoors was rapidly approaching, and wondering if we would be shot on the spot if we didn't make it home in time.

At school one day, an assembly was called. We were warned to keep a low profile as foreigners, and to stay at home as much as possible. Gradually, it became unsafe to travel to school on the bus and we were strongly advised to stay home. School was closed. We were effectively in lockdown.

I remember day after day, sitting in my bedroom, playing the guitar. I had no opportunity for guitar tuition, and had to be self-sufficient in my learning. It is this, I believe, that helped me become a more proficient player of the instrument; this period served me well in that respect.

During that year, I befriended an Iranian girl called Felor and we spent a lot of time together. She lived down the road, walking distance from my place. One day I went with my family to the lookout high above Tehran, in the Alborz mountains, for a picnic.

As I strolled five minutes away from my family to admire the view, a tall and bearded man who was standing near me began talking to me.

He said the view was wonderful, and that he was a university student in Tehran, and asked me where I was from. We chatted, and exchanged phone numbers.

A couple of days later we had spoken on the phone, deciding to meet in the big park in the city. Of course, I knew undoubtedly that my parents would never allow me to do such a thing, in a foreign city, with a total stranger, in the middle of a revolution.

But I was determined, and with my heart beating, told my parents I was going down the road to visit my friend Felor. Clutching the stranger's phone number and a few dollars, I left the house, walked down the street to a busy road and stood on the sidewalk, yelling out, 'Taxi!' When one pulled up, in I jumped, with two or three Iranian men, off into the big city. I alighted on a very busy road near the park. The tall stone walls of the park entrance was where we were to meet. It never once occurred to me that I might be unsafe, or land myself in trouble.

I felt tiny, standing there in the bright sunshine, against the massive stone walls, but also very powerful. Within minutes the man arrived. His name was Mahmood. He was older than me, and much, much taller. Had his plan been to bundle me into a car and take me to a village in the desert to be his wife, bear his children, never to set eyes on my family again, there is little I could have done.

The date was innocent. We talked, walked, and Mahmood held my hand. We bought ice-creams, and fed the ducks. We sat under a tree and he recited Persian poetry to me which was very beautiful in sound, and then translated.

At some stage we realised the day was fading and the sun was sinking. We caught a taxi back to my street, and we alighted at my corner. He insisted on walking me up the street to my house. When I arrived it was dark. My father opened the door, beside himself with rage.

He had rung Felor around lunchtime to enquire about me, and perplexed, she said she hadn't seen me for a week at least. Visions of disaster must have been flooding my father's mind, and rightfully so. We were in a foreign city, I didn't speak the language, and I had effectively disappeared. It was night and his daughter was nowhere to be found.

My father ordered me not to speak to Mahmood again. When foreigners had to leave Iran very quickly due to worsening conditions, my mother, my sister and I were due to board an Alitalia flight via Rome to Australia, while my father stayed on another few weeks.

I remember calling Mahmood, and with urgency, telling him we were leaving the country.

We arranged to meet at the airport, near the bathrooms. He arrived with an armful of red roses. Suddenly I felt a presence behind me and there was my father, grabbing the roses as they scattered on the floor, and saying to Mahmood, 'What do you want with my daughter? What are your intentions! Leave now!' Mahmood left in one direction, I in the other to board my flight, which was spent sobbing in heartbreak all the way to Rome. I thought I had lost the love of my life! What tragedy! In fact, I was a thirteen-year-old girl rushing across a huge city, alone, in the midst of a revolution, to meet a stranger, a man with whom I had spent less than an hour.

That was the last time I ever saw or spoke to him.

For the past six weeks we have been in what is referred to as 'lockdown'. I am grateful that years ago I already had the experience of lockdown. It is not unfamiliar, and in fact has aspects which are pleasant. Again, I sit and play guitar, day after day, as I did as a young girl in my room in Tehran in 1978...

Reflections on Home

...home is a gift...never to be taken for granted

Home has taken so many forms and meanings at various stages in my life. I found myself homeless after that disturbing home invasion. I could not return to my own place because at that time I felt too unsafe. I sought refuge at a women's shelter, and there I could fall asleep safe in the knowledge that I would not wake to someone standing over my bed, threatening my very being.

After I left the women's shelter I managed to secure some accommodation in the form of a tiny green wooden caravan that had formerly belonged to a rather eccentric French artist by the name of Jean-Pierre.

The caravan was my cocoon, it was warm and cosy, and at night I would light a candle, listen to soft music, slow my breath, and always sleep soundly after gently blowing out the candle and being enveloped in the still darkness. The morning light would be accompanied by the sound of chickens, so many of them, running about outside in the garden, ushering in the new day.

When I met my first love, the father of my children, we moved together to a small garage at the back of a house in Kingston in Canberra. It was simply four walls, a concrete floor, some rugs, a bed, and a small table with two chairs and a kettle and a small fridge, but it was home. It was home because there was love.

In Iran there was the very spacious, rambling apartment set around an internal courtyard. My favourite thing about it was the brilliant indigo blue and ruby red glass squares that made up the panels of the double doors leading to the lounge room. The light shone through them and their illuminated radiance was captivating. This was home, where I had my belongings, my family, my guitar, as the Revolution unfolded outside its walls.

There was a wonderfully exciting adventure to the tip of Australia, to Cape York, that occurred around the time I was living in Alice Springs where my sons were both born. My marriage had ended and I met a kind-hearted and impossibly handsome young man who was travelling around Australia. I experienced a shedding of my skin, threw all my belongings on the front lawn for sale, and headed with the young man, Rob, west to Mount Isa and then east to Cairns, following the coastline until we reached Cape York. Rob had fitted out the back of his four-wheel-drive to accommodate my sons, and built them a bed. They were ten months old and two years old. We bathed in clear emerald pools and under rushing waterfalls, walked lush tropical forests and vast untouched beaches, sat under starry skies around open fires at night. Freedom was mine for the taking. We slept in a tent, near a stream, a beach, or at a camp-site. We were home. I had my sons with me, I had love, I wrote in my journal every night, slept early and arose at the break of dawn... eventually, as young relationships often do, ours unravelled, and we parted ways, he to Sydney and I to Canberra.

Today was a freezing Autumn day with an Antarctic blast coming in from the south, bringing wind, rain and icy temperatures. All day my hands have been cold, and my nose icy. I ventured out to post a parcel, and outside the supermarket saw the homeless Russian man who sits each day with his dog, hoping for a few coins or notes. The dog was wrapped in two blankets, but the man, with whom I had chatted just a few days ago, looked frozen. I handed him a banana out of my shopping, which he ate immediately, and a ten dollar note. By the time I got to the post office it had dropped another couple of degrees in temperature. I was freezing. I went to the cafe and asked for the biggest cup available and ordered an extra hot hot-chocolate. It felt good on my cold hands as I carried it out of the building, back to the homeless man.

'Here,' I said, 'this will warm your hands, it's hot chocolate.'

He gratefully took it, wished me well, and as I left I saw the relief on his face as he wrapped his hands around the cup.

Those of us who can return home during the Covid-19 pandemic are fortunate. Those who can shelter from the elements, be it in a house, a tent, an apartment or a caravan are privileged. Those, such as the Russian man who for whatever reason finds himself homeless on this bitterly cold day, cannot.

Home is a gift, and never to be taken for granted.

My mother Maya wrote a book around her eightieth birthday called *The Silver Bracelet–an Egyptian Girlhood*. It was a treasured object on my bookshelf in Mallacoota, but was claimed by the fires. A few days ago she sent me a replacement copy. It was reassuring to hold it once again in my hands, a small homecoming... The book describes how the Suez Crisis forced foreigners, including my mother and her family, out of Egypt in 1956. Until that moment, Alexandria had been her home. My mother left for Paris during the Summer holidays only to realise once there, that she would never be returning home. Home no longer existed. She spent her life searching once more for home, until finally one day decades later, she rediscovered it in Alice Springs, Central Australia.

Perhaps writers' blood flows through our veins; or perhaps it is merely the fact that we both lost our homes, in completely different circumstances, that triggered our mutual desire to unravel through writing...

'The ache for home lives in all of us,
the safe place where we can go and not be questioned'
                                              Maya Angelou

MENAGERIE

we cherish them,
and the fact that they survived

Jim has returned from Mallacoota, where he needed to go quietly and on his own, to sift his way through the ash, and to see what remained if anything... This was Jim's closure: everybody reacts differently. I had no desire whatsoever to join him. He sent me photos of the devastation, and although there is some regrowth in some of the trees, it is still a surreal and barren scene, and I feel much sadness for what has been lost...

There was nothing much left in the ash that Jim could find, but he uncovered a small bronze frog which we bought together a few years ago. Another object to return with Jim to Canberra was a terracotta bird feeder which once attracted birds into our garden in Mallacoota. It now hangs from a tree in our garden in Canberra, and we take delight in our daily visitors: rosellas, cockatoos, wattle birds, and even hungry possums. There are other things that have remained with us, and are very special: a bass, a guitar, a small bag of sheet music containing my original songs and another couple of song folders, but most importantly, our surviving birds.

Blossom and Winston, our magnificent Alexandrines are resting now in Mallacoota; our stunning Romolo of red and yellow also at peace, and our cherished red-rumped parrots Sookie and Annie flying free, somewhere over the rainbow...

Here, we have nine birds which travelled with us to Brisbane and back: they are, in the order that they came into our lives, Olly, Polly, Pebble, Pepper, George, Rex, Sally, Peeps, and Ozzie. Gratefully, they are with us now, chirping merrily, each with their own unique idiosyncrasies...

Our lorikeets Peeps and Ozzie are flatmates: they tolerate each other, but make no effort to get to know each other better. Peeps was found in a park in Canberra by a friend, and she drove back to Mallacoota with Peeps on her shoulder, intending to keep him. That proved too much, so she called us asking if we would adopt him. Of course we agreed, and we named him Peeps because for a couple of weeks all we heard him say was *peep! peep!*

One afternoon we were driving back from the coast when, from the back of the Oka, we heard what sounded like a little terrier barking *woof!, woof!, woof!,* and then *come here! come here!* in a very Australian accent in a man's voice. For a moment, we didn't know where the sound was coming from, and then we realised it was Peeps saying *woof! woof! come here!, come here!,* and then, magically, he began a recital of birdcalls which was so expertly crafted in its imitation, as to have us believe that we were travelling with one seagull, a crow, a magpie, a lyrebird, a cuckoo and a pigeon... it was as though Peeps wanted to tell us all about his history, and needed a couple of weeks

to get to know us first... **Strangely enough, he** also could perfectly imitate an umpire's whistle, but his very favourite bird to imitate was and still is a black cockatoo. He reserves that for special occasions, and as the master actor that he is, has us truly captivated. Apart from that, he doesn't speak English. He is Jim's bird. They are very bonded, and Peeps will only come out and sit with Jim, on his shoulder, rarely with anyone else, and he'll fall asleep while Jim plays the bass. He also likes dancing and singing to music: he's a very musical bird. His preferred dining choices are baby spinach, and mincemeat, for which he goes crazy.

Ozzie, Peep's flatmate, was also a rescue bird. We drove to Geelong to pick him up, some four hours from Melbourne return, as he had been given away by family who had him for eight years, all his little life. We knew that he needed to go to a good loving home... From the moment we picked Ozzie up he bonded with me. We stopped back in Melbourne for the night, at a friend's place, and in the morning I let Ozzie out. He started playing with my shoelace, and looked up at me and said, 'Get me my warm drink!'

I said, 'Pardon?'

He said, 'I want my warm drink!'

'Okay,' I said, 'let's work out what this is all about,' so I rang the lady who had owned Ozzie and I said, 'What's this about a warm drink?'

She replied, 'That's what he calls his breakfast and dinner.'

'Oh, okay,' I said, 'That's interesting'...

Ozzie speaks complete sentences, grammatically correct, perfectly formulated, not words that we've taught him, just words that he's learnt and stored in his memory. Sometimes, more often at night, he begins to chatter and we pick up bits of his sentences, all sorts of things, such as, *'I want to go and stand on the balcony'* or *'I love the both of you'* or *'I'm going to destroy you'* or *'I want a cup of coffee'...* very well-formulated sentences. Ozzie is not an imitator, Ozzie has a whole language in his head, and brings it out when he's in the mood. Ozzie has a very favourite toy which is called a PEZ. It's a plastic orange toy with a dog's head (Pluto), and he drags it with him everywhere. He sleeps with it, and sometimes won't step out of his cage unless he steps onto the PEZ first. One of his favourite games is dragging the PEZ to the edge of the table and kicking it off so that it slides across the floor, then his human is supposed to pick it up and put it back on the table so he can do it all over again—cause-and-effect...

He has a red PEZ and a blue PEZ because his orange one is falling apart, but it won't do: he loves *his* orange one best. We even

managed to find a replacement orange one online with the same Pluto head and he even knows that that's not his trusty PEZ. He knows it's a replacement, just like a child would with a teddy bear...

Ozzie's choice of menu centres around 'birdycino'—when I make a cafe latte from our machine he will throw a tantrum if he doesn't have a little dish of foamy milk all for himself. He can't stand baby spinach, but practically dives head first into a teacup. He likes chamomile, orange and cinnamon, rosehip, chai, any type of tea as long as it's hot. One one would think that his tongue would burn but he just loves it, and his tongue is fine.

Then we have Olly, who used to be Polly. *She* is actually a *he*. When we acquired her with her older brother we thought she was a girl... Her older brother Papagai sadly passed away. Polly, now Olly, was out of sorts and very lonely for quite a while, after Papagai died, but then we found Percy... Percy was a Mallacoota bird, he was a baby and was being attacked. He refused to leave, even if the door was open, so ended up travelling with us, bonding with Olly and now they are best of friends. Percy, we discovered, is a girl so now her name is Polly. Polly and Olly are mates. Olly will eat almost anything that you offer him. He loves corn on the cob but as long as it's food it passes.

Then we have Pebble, a large, wild Mallacoota lorikeet who was at the animal shelter, as her tail had been ripped to bits by something, a fox perhaps, and she was and still is unable to fly. The wildlife shelter called us and asked if we would adopt her. Of course we agreed... She's a gentle soul, and has laid several eggs. Her partner is Pepper, he was also a Mallacoota baby with a little black beak, attacked by the flock and starving... We began to feed him and he also refused to leave, so we brought him travelling with us so he wouldn't starve.

We also have Rex or sexy Rex, which is his nickname. He's a very pale blue and white budgerigar who lived alone in a large aviary in a paddock in Mallacoota. He was very lonely and we adopted him so that he could have some company. His flatmates are George, a beautiful sky-blue budgerigar from Lakes Entrance, and Sally, a tiny lime-green and bright yellow budgerigar from Mullumbimby. George and Sally fell in love at first sight and have been faithful partners ever since. Rex doesn't get a look in with Sally, but he and George are firm friends and often have a good old afternoon chat: if they could, they would probably go down to the pub for a few beers every afternoon together.

And that is our bird family... we cherish them, and the fact that they survived. We also have acquired an assortment of magpies here in our new house, who arrive every afternoon for a little bit of company and food. There are also a large assortment of currawongs and their yellow mouthed babies with soft fluffy down. We look after them all, and we still make the weekly pilgrimage to the top of Red Hill, as we have done ever since we arrived in Canberra on that intensely hot smoky day in January, to care for our vagabond magpies on top of Red Hill who are very grateful for a few bites to eat and some water. They know us now and as soon as we park there, we are greeted enthusiastically by around thirty of them, begging and very happy to see us.

So, the bird life surrounding us is well, and we are grateful for our feathered friends. Not a day goes by that I don't think of our dear birds which perished in Mallacoota, and also for all the wildlife that was taken during that black summer of 2020....

REMNANTS

The feathers are beautiful but silent.

A new package arrives today at our door. It is addressed from our friend Leanne.

I open it. There are two books and a small painting of our bird Blossom. Carefully placed above the stack in a tidy arrangement, is a selection of feathers that once belonged to our deceased birds.

There is a gut-wrenching immediacy. Being thrown back with a jolt to pre-fire days where Winston, Blossom, Romolo, Sookie and Annie were loud, hungry, fluttering: and *alive*.

We look at each other in a strange kind of disbelief.

Slowly, carefully we pick up the feathers. There is a long slender green one, iridescent, that once was a part of Winston's tail, crucial in a bird's flight. There is a red, pale yellow and white feather; Romolo.

And the tiny opalescent feathers of Sookie and Annie...

I carry them tenderly and place them in a blue glass vase.

There is no chirping. The feathers are beautiful but silent.

They are remnants, simultaneously carrying us back to our Mallacoota Time, yet also serving to remind us that those days are a mere memory...

The Red Dog

...the bushfires left a mark

I met the red dog Smithie every Wednesday when I went to teach music to a friend. Smithie was a red heeler pup with impossibly large, pointy ears and intelligent black eyes. A cuter puppy would be hard to find. Smithie growled every time I was in his vicinity. He was an anxious dog. I learnt that Smithie also had been a bushfire victim on the South Coast, and sadly, had ended up at a shelter, where he had subsequently been rescued by my friend.

Smithie was about to commence dog obedience classes after his adoption, but suddenly, life changed for us all, including Smithie. The classes were cancelled and he stayed home, only going out for walks with his owner. He was unable to socialise with other dogs and lacked the experience of watching his owner socialise with other dog walkers.

Smithie, already anxious from former trauma, was further agitated and made fearful by Covid-19 restrictions, and its accompanying isolation.

I felt a bond with Smithie, because of our shared experiences...

Each week, as I was near Smithie, I observed a noticeable improvement in his acceptance of me, as he was able to tolerate sitting much closer to me and remain calm.

The last time I saw Smithie, he sat nearby for twenty minutes or so, then towards the end of our lesson he approached me and sniffed my leg.

I kept very still and calm, but suddenly out of the blue he lunged at me and snapped at my elbow, piercing the skin. My friend and his family were left shaken by the incident, as was I.

As I drove home, still feeling shocked from the bite, I wondered what unkown traumas poor Smithie had suffered. Unlike me, he couldn't write his feelings out or speak with a counsellor: but, like me, the bushfires left a mark on Smithie which was exacerbated by the arrival of Covid-19 and its accompanying restrictions.

It is worth remembering that trauma impacts animals also, not only humans. The bruise and pierced skin on my elbow serve as a reminder of that fact.

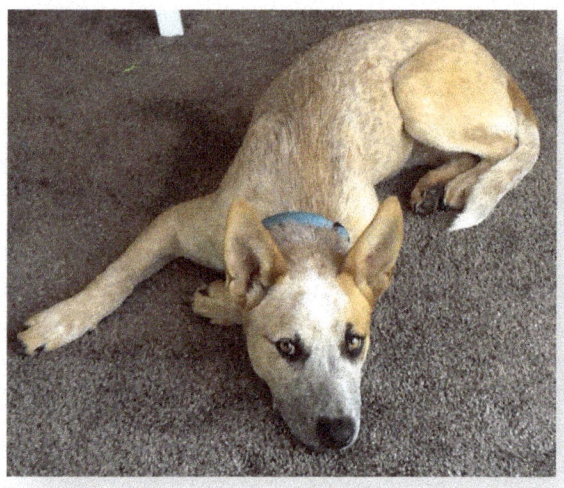

JULIE

It is not what is lost but what is gained...

It is part of the human condition to suffer loss. Loss visits our lives in many forms: one can lose a home, a marriage, gainful employment, a dear friend, one's mother or brother, one's innocence, one's sense of direction. One can lose one's senses, one's hearing, eyesight or sense of smell, one's mobility, sanity, sense of safety and certainty.

In the process of loss, often referred to as a dark night of the soul, one often receives revelatory gifts; in retrospect, as the fog of the dark night lifts, these are revealed. This process may take days, months or years, or may happen suddenly, in a lightning flash of realisation.

Julie danced into our lives on a deck at Tilba in the beautiful South Coast Hinterland whilst we were performing jazz at a cafe. She would have been seventy-five or so, but burst in like a sixteen-year-old ray of sunshine, spinning, twirling and laughing on the deck. She approached us, introduced herself and began chatting with us, then insisted on dragging anyone and everyone that came anywhere in our vicinity to meet us, and to tell them what wonderful music they were missing out on and that they *must* stay. From that day forward, Julie was a permanent fixture in our lives. She was a breath of fresh air and our biggest fan. Everywhere, anywhere we played, she was there, invariably insisting that a large crew of friends accompany her to listen to us.

Whenever we stopped in Narooma, Julie would insist that we come and stay with her in her enormous home, a house way too big for one elderly woman living alone. Downstairs was fitted out as a self-contained unit, and Julie would always place neatly folded towels and a chocolate at the foot of our bed, and ensure the small fridge was stocked with a little jug of milk, and the side table with two teacups and saucers, and teabags, just like any regular country motel would do.

Staying at Julie's was always a respite from the cramped quarters of the Oka, which was in itself quite comfortable but only to a point: after a couple of weeks the novelty would wear thin. Sojourns at Julie's did not come without a price: we could not get away without being subjected to the viewing of three hundred photographs that Julie had snapped, and each time we stayed, we would again be subjected to those three hundred photos, plus another thirty of her latest... it brought Julie immense happiness to share her life with us in this way. She took photos of everything, some were blurred, some crooked, most unremarkable, but to Julie they were an accurate representation of a very important moment in *her* day, a detailed record, so we nodded appreciatively at each one. We suffered through video footage as well, and I think we viewed her film of Morris dancers twenty times...

Julie had suffered breast cancer before we met her, and had undergone a double mastectomy. She had also lost her beloved husband and travel companion very suddenly to an aggressive stomach cancer which had claimed him from diagnosis to death in six short months. These were Julie's tremendous losses, and under her smiling exterior was a woman who had suffered her fair share of grief and loneliness.

A year or so after we met, Julie's cancer reappeared, metastasising to her lungs, and slowly but surely to her liver. She continued coming along to our shows and still managed her smiles and dances, but appeared thinner, and tired quickly. Her hair began to fall out in clumps, and her ankles would swell so that they appeared the same thickness as her calves. Julie was losing her appetite by the day, as dying people do; now, when we went to visit her I would make sure I cooked chicken and vegetable soup and I would sit by her side and feed her small spoonfuls, and offer her sips of water. Jim would sit at her feet on the carpet, unbandage her thick ankles, and gently massage her feet and legs to try and encourage drainage and circulatory flow.

One evening she bid us goodnight and shuffled to her bedroom. After half an hour or so I noticed the light was still on in her room, so I went in, and found her sitting on the edge of her bed, half undressed, looking utterly dejected. I asked her what was wrong. She had taken a sleeping tablet before dinner and it had kicked in while she was getting undressed. She had no physical or mental energy to get undressed and put herself to bed, so we helped her into her nightgown and put her to bed, tucking her in like a small child and turning out the light.

One day, a few weeks later, Julie called me and asked if we would be interested in performing a concert at her home. She explained that she was unable to go out anymore and missed our music. Her biggest loves had been travel, with her husband, around Australia, and going to watch live music.

'I can't come to you, but will you come to me?' she asked.

I accepted without hesitation. The day of the concert arrived and Julie had invited fifty or so of her closest friends. The house was filled with fresh flowers. We performed, just for Julie; as far as I was concerned she was the only person in the room. I sang the song that she had first danced to, on the deck: *All of Me*, and when I sang *Raining on the Rock* she began to cry as she recalled her travels with her husband to the Red Centre.

There were flowers, tears, laughter, the house bursting with love.

That was Julie's farewell concert: two days later I spoke with her briefly on the phone and she passed away the following morning.

The loss of Julie revealed to me how quickly those we cherish can pass before our eyes, and that we must celebrate those we love while they are here to appreciate it. The most loving eulogy spoken too late will fall on deaf ears for the person it is meant for. The time to celebrate the people we love, the time to say in plain words *I love you,* the time to hug those close to you and say *you matter to me,* is *now.* This is the lesson in loss. The loss of Mallacoota was even more sudden than that of Julie's, but there can be drawn a parallel of my love for Julie, and the love for my home in Mallacoota: both were lost without much warning, and both left me bereft. The loss of Mallacoota taught me, as Julie's loss did, that the present moment is that which is to be cherished, because tomorrow may never come. Now is your moment in the sun.

Moment In The Sun
Don't you think it's time
to kick back and unwind
put your feet up
close the door
think about a little less
a little more,

Your mind is like a garden
your thoughts are the seeds
the harvest you reap
can be flowers or weeds

It's a brand new day,
everything might go your way
At times the clouds can block the sun
and days seem dark
you've lost your spark

Your mind is like a garden
your thoughts are the seeds
the harvest you reap
can be flowers or weeds
Now's your moment in the sun
tomorrow may never come

Find your river
Go for a row
You've been going way too fast
Time to go slow
Find your mountain go for a climb
leave your cares far behind

Reach out and hold someone's hand
lay together in the sand
open up and say I love you
Now's your moment in the sun
Tomorrow may never come...

Your mind is like a garden
your thoughts are the seeds
the harvest you reap
can be flowers or weeds
Now's your moment in the sun
tomorrow may never come

THE SNAKE TRACK

And now, today, salt in our wounds.

Today, we received the surreal news that Jim's forty-acre property at Kiah NSW, on the Snake Track, was totally destroyed by the January bushfires.

We had not had a chance to return there after December as we were in Brisbane when our home in Mallacoota was taken. Jim's property and little shack would have to wait. We always imagined that as we had heard nothing it had most likely survived the fires. But this fire was a ravenous one. If there was dry bush to consume, consume it, it would.

Up in flames went Jim's shack, where he raised four children, up in flames went his Ducati motorcycle, all his tools and personal belongings and my treasures that I had placed into storage there. My diaries; a lifetime of secrets, longings and musings recorded from the time I was twelve or so. My books, so many of them, each one cherished; guitar music and CDs. All my photography albums containing my babies' first smiles; picnics with friends; travels in Italy; summers at the coast with my family; wedding photos; photos of my children's birthday parties. A book I had written, my first ever; when I was seven years old, titled *The Lonely Doll*; proud was I to be asked to walk around school and show the other classes my writing. I wanted to hand that book, written in careful seven-year-old handwriting, to my granddaughters. But it was not to be.

Today, four months after the bushfires, we learnt that even The Snake Track is gone, the incessant call of the bellbirds silenced. And as our Mallacoota wounds were slowly beginning to heal, this terrible news reopened them, and salt was added, as we tried to make sense once again of the enormous loss that we and countless others around Australia dealt with and are dealing with still, after *The Lost Summer*...

Pilgrimage

... kindnesses have lifted me, sustained me

So, Jim returns from his pilgrimage to Mallacoota, dusty and drained. He says that he is glad that he spent three days systematically rummaging through the ash and cutting up roof metal to see what was buried underneath. He says it has bought him a sense of closure, and for that I'm happy...

The stories I hear make my heart ache. Jim tells me of blackened trees, of the absence of kookaburra calls in the morning and the afternoon. He tells me of the lack of koalas and kangaroos. All of this makes me very sad.

Mallacoota is in lockdown, and normally at this time of year it is rampant with tourists, the van park overflowing, but Jim tells me there is nobody about. He has taken photos of our place and surrounding landscapes, and I sit and stare at them in disbelief. The photos that he brings back seem to hit me harder than those I took when we both went back to Mallacoota on the 9th of February. These photos seem more real to me, and they bring home like a rude slap the fact that everything is gone.

Jim returns with a few tools and the bronze frog which we bought together a few years ago. The frog has changed colour, fired by the violent flames, and then buried in the rubble, but it is a survivor. Strangely, in that intensely hot and ferocious firestorm,

the survivors on our block have been an odd assortment of frogs: one made of bronze, a glazed green ceramic one, one small pottery one and a large clay one. So, these five frogs have hopped their way into our new life in Canberra... They have banded together, the frog survivors. Jim recounts how on the last day in Mallacoota a frog came and jumped into his hand. It was the size of his palm and they had a bit of a chat: another survivor...

The Grocon cleanup team are in Mallacoota systematically working through the destroyed homes, around one hundred and fifty in total, that need to be cleaned up so that the rebuilding process can begin. One of the Grocon workers, a young man, noticed Jim working tirelessly from morning till night digging through the rubble. He came and stopped by, insisting that Jim share half of his tuna lunch, and made him a tuna sandwich.

Again and again, over the course of my journey towards recovery, I have returned to this simple yet powerful realisation: that people are kind. I am awed. These kindnesses have lifted me, sustained me, and contribute toward the rebuilding of my self...

I have made contact with a social worker who will replace the psychologist that I was initially going to see, but with whom I did not gel whatsoever. I've chatted to this social worker on the phone and she sounds quite compatible with me. She told me I didn't have to share anything and I could be really careful and tread lightly. She explained that she's a trauma expert. No! I don't need to tread lightly! I feel like I need to dump everything I have felt in these past few months on her, and to allow her to help me unravel whatever needs to be unravelled...

The land in Mallacoota may or may not sell, or may take a long time, as COVID-19 has created a large slump in the economy: first there was the bushfire crisis, then the Covid-19 crisis and Australia is suffering deeply. It may take years for the scars to heal. If and when our land sells, we will decide where to go, what to do, what direction to take; perhaps life will reveal the right path, if there is such a thing. I have mixed feelings about leaving Mallacoota; I feel such grief at having to let it all go, but at the same time I could never go back. Things will never be the same... Indeed, globally, the world has changed: a world where people cannot hug for many months is a changed world. There are so many uncertainties that lie ahead. We don't know much about

this virus and how it will play out, we don't know exactly how the economy will be affected and what the repercussions will be...

Personally, we don't know exactly where home will be. There is one image that Jim took with his camera that haunts me, and it is that of the incinerated, tortured metal of the cage that belonged to Blossom and Winston... I cannot fathom what they went through, but the cage speaks volumes. Jim says that the windows at the front of the house were just globules of melted glass, and that our beautifully engraved brass Tibetan singing bowl has melted beyond belief. Our hearts have melted beyond belief also, but over time they will heal and perhaps resonate in harmony again like the singing bowl once did, and we will move forward from this black summer...

I hope to go to Mallacoota again with Jim, when I feel ready, driving the familiar snaking road through the forest regrowth. I hope to see lyrebirds and wallabies, and to hear kookaburras calling each other through the eucalypts. I hope to sit on the beach and watch the changing light. I hope to go and visit friends who have lost their homes, and to be able to share cups of tea and long hugs... I hope to sail again on the lake, and see black swans. I hope to go to Lucy's, the best dumpling house in Australia, and feast on her dumplings. I hope to bring our music back to Mallacoota and to write some songs which may contribute to people's healing.

I hope that the next place we live in will be as beautiful as Mallacoota was, although I don't know if such a place exists... I hope that Mallacoota will recover her beauty, and heal, rising above the ashes. Jim's trip to Mallacoota has bought us both a bittersweet closure: we must let go, surrender, and accept what has happened... Indeed, in life, letting go is essential for healing, for it is there, in that space of acceptance, that healing can truly begin to take place.

Supposing

... for home is not four walls

Supposing 11 Betka Road Mallacoota hadn't burnt down on New Year's Eve 2019... Suppose we had returned from Brisbane, as planned, after our Christmas reunion, to find our little cedar cottage sitting there, happily waiting for our return... suppose the birds were chirping, welcoming us in their assortment of unique ways, and Aristotle was snorting in the tree out the front, or perhaps, dozing, oblivious to our return...

Supposing we had walked in, put our bags down, and made a cup of tea, sat on our red couch, or perhaps our old blue couch on the front verandah, and discussed a few Christmas memories, shared a few laughs, perhaps a few songs...

Supposing the weeks had rolled into months and maybe years, and we returned to our life of travelling from Mallacoota back and forth, in our Oka, as we had always done, playing music up and down the coastline. Returning always to our safe haven for some restful down time, re-connecting with nature and with our birds, our constant backdrop the gentle hum of the ocean...

Would that have been our perfect life? Would we have remained there, in that cycle, for years to come? Or at some point, would we have decided that the time had come for a change? Perhaps circumstances may have directed us elsewhere? Perhaps we might have made the decision to move closer to a hospital because of Jim's medical issues, or perhaps to be closer to our granddaughters Willow and Violet... It is feasible that at some stage we may have decided that, as much as we love Mallacoota, it is time to move on...

We would have had to go through the motions of sorting our things into piles to keep, give or throw away; we would have had to acquire boxes and carefully pack our belongings. We would have had to spend a huge amount of time and energy in that process, and also in the process of deciding where to go and what to do next...

Supposing we had moved to an entirely new location, leaving Mallacoota behind apart from perhaps the occasional visit... Mallacoota would have become an opaque, much cherished memory, a place where we had felt at ease, a place where the beauty took our breath away each day, where the wildlife stopped by to say hello, a place where friends were always welcome and our door was always open, where we shared food, music and laughter with all who came through the door... where the green golden afternoon light filtered through the tall eucalypts as the myriad of birds who perched in those trees sang in unison in perfect bird harmony; a place where love filled the walls: a place we called home...

I don't know yet where home will be... home might be near the ocean, in a little cedar cottage with tall eucalypts and our very own koala; home might be a rambling four bedroom brick house in a leafy Canberra suburb, waking to the currawongs' song and the cockatoos passing by overhead... or perhaps a large apartment overlooking a park somewhere... it might be an acre or two on the South Coast with an apple orchard, beehives, and an aviary, or even a houseboat on an impossibly wide river in the direction of North...

Yet, when we find ourselves in that place that resonates, as Mallacoota did all those years ago, and when we walk up to that door, wherever that door may be, and we look at each other and say *we are home*, then undoubtedly, surely, that home will be filled with music and friends, laughter and love; for home is not four walls, but what is contained within those walls... And wherever we wander, those gifts that life offers us will resonate within our walls, and amplify our lives.

And that is the lesson of our Mallacoota Time...

Slow Easy Change

I feel a slow kind of easy change coming over me
I feel a cool breeze blowing through my open heart
I hear a voice of wisdom and it's calling me
And I know, everything will be alright
Things are just fine.
I see a light shining
on the distant horizon.
I sense a new day dawning
and it's just begun
I see blue sky showing
through the stormy clouds
And I know everything will be alright
Things are just fine.
What goes around must come around
Just takes time to see that view
What you give is what you get
Give it time you'll know it's true
I can hear but I choose to listen
I can touch but I choose to feel
I can look but I choose to see
I can be,
I can be me.
I feel the sunshine warming up my sleepy soul
I feel a new song stirring in my tired bones
I hear the heartbeat of a drum start to roll,
And I know,
Everything will be alright,
Things are just fine,
Things are just fine...

www.ingramcontent.com/pod-product-compliance
Lightning Source LLC
Chambersburg PA
CBHW061305110426
42742CB00012BA/2069